101

Black Inventors
and their Inventions

Joy James

First Printed in United Kingdom 2021

Published by Conscious Dreams Publishing
www.consciousdreamspublishing.com

Edited by Elise Abram

Typeset by Oksana Kosovan

ISBN: 978-1-913674-39-7

Dedication

For Milton, Jade, and Jules who inspire me.

Preface

This book was an idea long before I started writing it. When my children were younger, I wanted a book about Black role models to help inspire them and expand their little minds. I knew this information was out there somewhere, but I could not find anything in an organised format or the form of a children's book. I hope that people young and old will enjoy reading about the many Black inventors in our world and their wonderful contributions that help to improve our lives. I hope that they will be heartened by this. Our world has certainly benefitted from these amazing inventions!

Contents

Introduction

This book looks at 101 Black inventors, but there are so many more. These are the men and women who often had to fight against the odds to have their inventions come to fruition and be recognised.

You will notice that many of the inventors are from America, and this is because of a man named Henry Baker who was working in the US Patent Office at a time when inventions by Black inventors were credited to others due to discrimination and racial inequality. Henry wanted to make sure that these inventors were properly recognised for their achievements, so he decided to research and document their information. Some of these inventors gave permission to reveal their identities, while others were worried this might affect the success of their inventions.

There is very little information available about Black inventors in the UK and other countries, and this is simply because the patent offices do not state whether an inventor is Black. In the end, it is of less relevance where these inventors were born than the greater significance of the history of Black people in the world.

For younger readers, a note to explain that patents protect inventions from being copied by someone else without your permission, so inventors usually register their invention at patent offices to stop someone else from trying to take credit for their inventions.

Some inventions in this book are simple designs we use every day with little thought as to what life might be like without them, while others are mind-boggling creations. Although this book assigns one main invention to each inventor, most of them have created many other inventions. This book celebrates them all!

MARGARET (MAGGIE) ADERIN-POCOCK

Wind Speed Monitor

Dr Margaret Aderin-Pocock is a space scientist, science expert and educator who invented the wind speed monitor.

She was born in 1968 in London, UK, to Nigerian parents. Margaret, known as Maggie, was interested in space from a very young age. She saved up to buy a telescope, which she improved by adding motors, software, and electronics, and after that she was able to track faraway stars with it.

Maggie was also interested in science. She received a bachelor's degree in physics and a doctorate in mechanical engineering from Imperial College London.

Her telescope inspired her to work on related projects, including NASA's (National Aeronautics and Space Administration) James Webb Space Telescope, the Gemini Observatory in Hawaii, US, and ESA's (European Space Agency) Earth Explorer Atmospheric Dynamics Mission satellite, Aeolus.

Maggie has invented instruments for both industrial and academic environments, ranging from handheld landmine detectors to systems designed to monitor wind speeds and other variables in the Earth's atmosphere. These instruments help in the fight against climate change on our planet. She also built a spectrograph instrument for the Gemini South Telescope in Chile, which allows scientists to examine the light from stars to learn more about them, such as the chemical reactions that take place deep inside them.

She received an MBE (Member of the Most Excellent Order of the British Empire), awarded by the Queen, for services to science and education in 2009. Maggie is a presenter on the BBC (British Broadcasting Corporation) television show *The Sky at Night* and has been a science consultant on many television programmes.

She is the founder of Science Innovation Ltd, which organises events to engage children and adults in the wonders of space science.

DOUNNE ALEXANDER

Natural Health Foods

Dounne Alexander is a pioneering businesswoman who created natural health foods.

She was born in 1949 in Trinidad in the Caribbean and came to the UK with her family in 1962, at the age of 15. She worked as a chemical technician and housing officer for many years.

In 1987, Dounne decided on a career change when she noticed a growing trend in natural health foods. She pioneered in this trend when she began to put into practice valuable life lessons learnt in the Caribbean from when she was young, around family values, health, and longevity.

She blended natural foods with medicinal and culinary herbs to support natural healing processes and maintain optimum health. Dounne established her herbal food manufacturing business, called *Gramma's Herbal Foods*, in memory of her grandmother, who lived a long and healthy life until the age of 113.

Within just a few months, she was selling her natural health foods in high-end retail outlets in London, including Harrods, Selfridges, and Fortnum and Mason. She also got her products on the shelves of the top seven supermarket chains, including Waitrose, Tesco, and Safeway. In 2008, her herbal products were approved for use in hospital and hospice palliative care programmes (specialised medical care for people with serious illnesses).

Her range of health food products includes herbal seasonings and a selection of herbal teas and drinks. She has won many national awards, including 'Women Mean Business' and 'Black Businesswoman of the Millennium.'

In 2007, Dounne received an MBE (Member of the Most Excellent Order of the British Empire), awarded by the Queen, for outstanding service in the British food industry.

VIRGIE AMMONS

Fireplace Damper Tool

Virgie Ammons was a caretaker who invented a tool to open and close a fireplace damper (a cover at the top of the fireplace where it joins the chimney).

Virgie was born in 1908 in Maryland, US. She moved to West Virginia where she worked as a caretaker, looking after and maintaining properties.

Her invention fixed the problem of fireplace dampers that flutter and make a noise when strong winds come down the chimney. A damper allows smoke and gases from a fireplace to escape through the chimney, so it must be open when there is a fire burning. It also helps to keep out cold air, rain, debris and animals when closed, once the fire is fully out.

Some dampers do not stay all the way closed, and Virgie was concerned this could cause loss of heat in the winter, which wastes energy. Her invention controls the opening and closing of the damper and allows it to stay fully closed when the fireplace is not in use.

Virgie died in 2000 in West Virginia at the age of 91.

LISA ASCOLESE

Luggage Assistant

Lisa Ascolese is an entrepreneur, mentor and motivational speaker who invented the luggage assistant.

She was born in London, UK, grew up in New York, US, and studied computer science at Brooklyn College in New York. Lisa started inventing at the age of nine when she created glue-tipped shoelaces to stop them from becoming untied.

She patented her luggage assistant invention in 2016, a device that holds a suitcase securely while travelling. She also patented a hanger cover in 2017 that gives better protection to clothing on hangers, and is widely used in the professional laundering services industry.

Lisa is the founder of Inventing A to Z, a product development company that helps people who want to create and develop their own products. She has successfully created, patented, marketed, and launched many products on television channels QVC (Quality Value Convenience) and HSN (Home Shopping Network), as well as in retail stores.

Known as 'The Inventress', she also founded the Association of Women Inventors and Entrepreneurs, where she has been taking ideas – hers and those of others – from start to fruition for many years. She organises conferences to bring together and inspire women inventors and help with inventions in categories such as mother care nursing products, kitchen organisers, and hair accessories.

Lisa says that 'a good invention is something everybody needs. Create a solution to a problem everybody has. Every day, something happens in life where you modify something. Problem, modification, invention.'

ALEXANDER ASHBOURNE

Biscuit Shape Cutter

Alexander Ashbourne was a caterer and grocery store owner who invented the biscuit shape cutter.

Born in 1820 in Pennsylvania, US, he grew up cutting wheat on a farm and began to think of more efficient ways to make harvesting easier. This was the start of Alexander's inventions.

As a young adult, he became a well-known and respected caterer, providing food for weddings and buffets in Philadelphia, and was one of a handful of local caterers selected for the Emancipation Celebration in 1863. While working at this event, Alexander noticed that the biscuits were formed by hand and were not uniform in shape. This inspired him to design an industrial biscuit shape cutting device.

Over the next decade, he worked on creating a spring-loaded biscuit shape cutter that would guarantee a uniform shape and size for big batches of biscuits. His design was patented in 1876 and consisted of a large board that helped to load and unload biscuits easily. There were large metal plates with various shapes, which could be pushed down to cut the dough. His invention revolutionised the baking industry all over the world.

Alexander continued to invent other things, and he received a patent for processing coconut oil in 1877, which he had developed over three years. The Ashbourne process for refining coconut oil ensured that no unsaturated fatty acids remained, and the refined oil was used in food products and hair and beauty products.

He died in 1915 in California at the age of 95.

LEONARD BAILEY

Folding Bed

Leonard Bailey was a business owner and inventor of the folding bed.

He was born in 1825 and lived in Washington, DC, US. Leonard worked as a barber and built up a string of successful barbershops by the time of the American Civil War (1861-1865).

He was a member of the first mixed-race jury in Washington, DC in 1869. By the 1880s, he was an established leader of Washington, DC's Black business community.

In 1888, Leonard helped to set up the Capitol Savings Bank, one of the first Black-owned banks in the US, to provide affordable loans and insurance for the poorer households in the district. By 1893, during one of the country's worst financial crises, the Capitol Savings Bank was one of the few banks in Washington, DC that continued to stay in business.

Leonard received patents for several inventions. In 1899, he invented a folding bed, which was recommended to the US Army Medical Board for tent and camping purposes. He also invented the rapid mail-stamping machine, and a device to move trains to different tracks.

These inventions provided him with a good income. He continued to be successful in his community and served on the board of directors of the Manassas Industrial School for Coloured Youth in Virginia, where a residence hall was named after him.

Leonard died in 1918 in Maryland at the age of 92.

BENJAMIN BANNEKER

Farm Irrigation System

Benjamin Banneker was a self-taught astronomer, writer, mathematician, and building surveyor who devised a farm irrigation system to help keep plants and crops watered.

He was born in 1731 in Maryland, US. Benjamin received little schooling, but he enjoyed maths, science, and music and spent his time farming, studying, and reading.

He constructed an irrigation system for the 100-acre family farm on which he grew up, and which he later came to own. He built ditches and small dams to control water from the spring (known as Bannaky Spring) on the farm. Benjamin cultivated tobacco, and his tobacco farm flourished, even during times of drought.

In 1753, he created a wooden clock after a neighbour had loaned him a pocket watch. He took apart the watch and studied the parts closely before putting it back together and building his own clock, which was made entirely out of wood and kept accurate time for the rest of his life.

In 1791, Benjamin's talents led to his involvement in surveying territory and planning the construction of the capital city of Washington, DC.

From 1792 to 1797, he became an active writer and published six almanacs (annual handbooks). They sold very well and included his astronomical calculations, editorials, literature, and medical and tidal information, which was useful to fishermen.

Benjamin died in 1806 in Maryland at the age of 74.

WILLIAM HARRY BARNES

Hypophyscope

Dr William Harry Barnes was an otolaryngologist (ear, nose, and throat doctor) who invented the hypophyscope, a medical device used by neurosurgeons to find the pituitary gland in the brain.

William was born in 1887 in Pennsylvania, US. He knew that he wanted to be a doctor from an early age.

He completed his studies at the University of Pennsylvania Medical School in 1912, specialising in otolaryngology, which deals with conditions of the head and neck.

Throughout his career, William constantly developed new and improved surgical techniques, including simplified procedures for treating tumour growths in the ear, nose, and throat. By the 1930s, he had expanded his expertise to include laryngology and broncho-esophagology, which are areas of medicine focused on the lungs, airways, voice box, vocal cords and windpipe.

His invention of the hypophyscope allowed neurosurgeons to find and operate on the pituitary gland more easily. The pea-sized pituitary gland is found on the underside of the brain and is important for general health and wellbeing. It regulates vital body functions and controls the activity of most other glands, which secrete hormones directly into the bloodstream, and this, in turn, affects many different processes in the body.

William also perfected a way to remove a patient's tonsils in just ten minutes with little to no bleeding.

He died in 1945 in Pennsylvania at the age of 58.

JANET EMERSON BASHEN

LinkLine Software

Janet Emerson Bashen is an entrepreneur and business consultant who invented a software programme called LinkLine, which helps businesses organise their documents. She was the first Black woman to receive a patent for a software invention.

Janet was born in 1957 in Ohio, US. She was raised in Alabama, which inspired a lifelong quest to try to understand the country's history and struggle with issues of race.

She earned a bachelor's degree in legal studies and government at the University of Houston in Texas, a master's degree in labour and employment law at Tulane Law School in Louisiana, and completed postgraduate studies at Rice University in Texas.

Janet is the founder of the Bashen Corporation, a human resources consulting firm which she set up in 1994. The demand for their services led her to design LinkLine, a web-based application case management software for investigations in equal employment opportunity complaints about discrimination in the workplace. The software programme, patented in 2006, was a way to simplify claims tracking and document management relating to these complaints.

She has since developed additional tools to strengthen and support diversity in the workplace.

Janet has also written many articles and papers about equal employment opportunities, diversity, and fair employment practices.

PATRICIA ERA BATH
Laserphaco Probe

Dr Patricia Era Bath was an ophthalmologist (medical eye specialist) and inventor of the Laserphaco Probe, a surgical tool that uses a laser to remove cataracts (a condition where the lens of the eye becomes cloudy and affects vision) to help restore eyesight. She became the first woman to receive a medical patent for her invention.

Patricia was born in 1942 in New York, US. She received a medical degree from Howard University in Washington, DC, followed by an internship at Harlem Hospital. In 1973, she was the first Black woman to complete a residency in ophthalmology in the US.

She did further work at Columbia University in New York, where she found that Black people were twice as likely to suffer from blindness and eight times more likely to develop glaucoma than other patients. Her research led to the development of a community ophthalmology system, which provided eye care to those who were not able to afford treatment.

In 1976, Patricia co-founded the American Institute for the Prevention of Blindness, which established that 'eyesight is a basic human right.'

In 1988, she invented the Laserphaco Probe, which has revolutionised the treatment of cataracts. The device uses laser technology to treat cataracts in a less painful and more precise way, and Patricia has helped to restore the sight of people who had been blind for more than 30 years.

Among her many roles in the medical field, she was also a strong advocate of telemedicine, which uses technology to provide medical services in remote areas.

Patricia died in 2019 in California at the age of 76.

ANDREW JACKSON BEARD

Railway Carriage Coupler (improvement)

Andrew Jackson Beard invented improvements to the railway carriage coupler, which joins carriages together.

Andrew was born in 1849 in Alabama, US. He had no formal schooling and was a farmer, carpenter, blacksmith, railway worker, and businessman, as well as an inventor.

As a farmer, his work in agriculture led to his improvement of the double plough in 1884, which allowed the distance between the plough plates to be adjusted. He patented a second plough in 1887, which allowed the pitch angle of the plough blades to be adjusted. Ploughs are used by farmers to turn the soil before sowing seeds or planting crops.

In 1897, Andrew patented an improvement to railway carriage couplers, called the Jenny Coupler, which automatically hooked railway carriages together. Before that, this used to be done manually by placing a pin in a link between two carriages, which was extremely dangerous and he himself lost a leg in such an accident. He received three patents for automatic carriage couplers, which the government insisted railway companies use for health and safety reasons. His invention revolutionised railway safety.

He profited from his inventions, which allowed him to spend his time working on more inventions. He also invested in a successful real estate business.

Andrew died in 1921 in West Virginia at the age of 71.

GEORGE BECKET

Front Door Letterbox

George Becket designed the front door letterbox, a mail slot permanently mounted on the front door of a house.

George was living in Rhode Island, US, when he patented his front door letterbox invention in 1892.

In the early 1800s, people had to pick up their mail from the post office. From 1863, the post office started to deliver mail to the homes of people who lived in cities. By 1890, most cities delivered mail to people's homes, which led to the need for mailboxes.

George's front door letterbox invention was an inexpensive and safe letter holder, consisting of a frame and a self-closing box or container with a hinged opening, which was mounted to the front door of a house. Today, almost all front doors use his letterbox design.

EARL BELL

Slide Skin Seat

Earl Bell is a building designer and architectural design consultant who invented the slide skin seat, an ergonomic chair system that supports and moves with the person sitting in it.

Earl was born in 1977 in New York, US. His passion for science and design began at a very young age.

He thought of his first invention at the age of nine when he made friends with a spider and fed it insects to watch how it used its web as a home and to get food. This led to his idea, called Spidertecture, which was a tower made of pods that looked like a spider's web, and it later formed the basis for his design of the Afri Tower in Johannesburg, South Africa.

Earl studied architecture at Arkansas State University and began documenting his inventions while attending the Pratt Institute in New York in 1998.

His inventions include the charge ring to charge electric cars, exo-structural panels to provide structural support to buildings, and Sasu Technology – a liquid hydraulic electrical display for showing information, similar to an LCD (liquid crystal display) screen.

Earl's slide skin seat was patented in 2004. He made this unique seating system out of magnesium tubing, fabric, and small, easily detachable mechanical devices. The fabric is attached to the tubing in such a way that it slides easily on and off. The design was inspired by the science of human skeletal mechanics and innovative fabric construction.

He also designed the Buna Table, which is a table shaped like a pyramid standing on its point. It was originally an architectural design, but he found that it was better suited as a table.

MIRIAM ELIZABETH BENJAMIN

Gong and Signal Chair/Call Button System

Miriam Elizabeth Benjamin was a schoolteacher who invented the gong and signal chair or call button system. She became the second Black woman to receive a US patent for her invention.

Miriam was born in 1861 in South Carolina, US. Her family moved to Massachusetts in the early 1870s. She then moved to Washington, DC in the 1880s, where she worked as a schoolteacher.

Her gong and signal chair invention added to the convenience and comfort of guests at hotels who used to have to call out loud for assistance or clap their hands to get the attention of wait staff or attendants. The guest pressed a small button on the back of the chair, which sounded the gong for attention. A light also lit up, allowing the attendant to see which guest needed help.

Her invention was patented in 1888 and provided the basis for the call button system used nowadays on aeroplanes, for passengers seeking assistance from flight attendants. It is a key tool for customer service in the airline industry.

Miriam went on to study medicine and law at Howard University in Washington, DC. She returned to Massachusetts where she worked as a solicitor in patents for her brother, a well-known lawyer at the time, who owned a law firm.

In 1917, she patented a system to deliver medication via inserts in the sole of a shoe. She also had success composing marches under the pseudonym EB Miriam, one of which was used by Theodore Roosevelt's US presidential campaign in 1904.

Miriam died in 1947 in Massachusetts at the age of 85.

LEONIDAS HARRIS BERRY

Eder-Berry Biopsy Gastroscope

Dr Leonidas Harris Berry was a gastroenterologist (digestive system doctor) who invented the Eder-Berry biopsy gastroscope, which made it easier for doctors to collect tissue from the inside of the stomach without surgery.

Leonidas was born in 1902 in North Carolina, US. He received his bachelor's degree from Wilberforce University in Ohio in 1924. He went on to receive a second bachelor's degree in 1925 and a doctor of medicine degree in 1929 from the University of Chicago in Illinois. He also received a master's degree in pathology from the Graduate School of Medicine at the University of Illinois in 1933.

In 1934, he became a junior attending doctor in gastroenterology at Provident Hospital in Illinois, which was the first Black-owned hospital in the US. In 1946, he became the first Black attending doctor at Cook County Hospital in Illinois.

Leonidas spent most of his life studying the lining of the stomachs of alcoholics. In 1955, he invented the Eder-Berry biopsy gastroscope, the first direct-vision suction instrument used for taking tissue samples from the stomach. His pioneering work showed that it was the livers of alcoholics that were diseased and not their stomachs, which revolutionised the diagnosis and treatment of alcoholism.

His work focused on the physical and social welfare of people, and he was passionate about finding ways to educate the Black community on health. He wrote many books and articles on this and received many awards for his work.

Leonidas died in 1995 in Illinois at the age of 93.

JAK BEULA (JOHNNY ALEXANDER BUBEULA DODD)

Board Game (Nubian Jak)

Jak Beula is an entrepreneur who designed the board game *Nubian Jak*.

He was born Johnny Alexander Bubeula Dodd in 1963 in London, UK, to Jamaican parents. Jak is also a writer, jazz musician, singer, songwriter, sculptor, cultural activist, educator, former model, and social worker.

After working with some young people who felt dissatisfied with life and rejected by society, Jak decided to find a way to help them look at positive role models of Black heritage in the UK and Europe. In 1994, He created a board game called *Nubian Jak* to help young people gain knowledge of Black historical facts. The game combines questions on historical facts with pop trivia to highlight some of the achievements of Black people.

Nubian Jak was officially launched at the British Toy and Hobby Fair in 1995 and was recognised as one of the top ten games at the time. It was introduced at Hamleys, a multinational toy store, and this coincided with a Christmas marketing campaign on radio stations. Within a few weeks, the game was outselling the board game *Monopoly* and is described as the 'Black Trivial Pursuit'.

In 1996, a different version of Jak's board game was released at the New York International Toy Fair, which looked at Black people's achievements worldwide and not just in the UK and Europe. In 2000, the game's success was followed by the Millennium Declaration Edition. In 2006, the International Anniversary Edition was issued in honour of ten years of sales, and in 2009, the special US limited edition was released in honour of the election of President Barack Obama. This has made *Nubian Jak* the most successful series of games today.

Jak's board game has won many awards. He has also created a deck of cards, a computer game, and written a book on the *Nubian Jak* theme. In 2016, a *Nubian Jak* phone app was released.

HENRY BLAIR

Corn Planter

Henry Blair was a farmer who invented the corn planter. He was the second Black person to receive a US patent for his invention.

Born in 1807 in Maryland, US, Henry was a successful farmer who invented new devices to assist with the planting and harvesting of crops, which increased productivity and efficiency in farming.

His first patent in 1834 was for a corn planter, which was a type of wheelbarrow with a compartment to hold the seeds, and rakes dragging behind it to cover the seeds as they were dropped into the ground. This device meant that farmers could plant more corn more easily and in less time.

His second patent was for a cotton planter in 1836. This device worked by splitting the ground with two shovel-like blades that were pulled along by a horse or other farm animal. A wheel-driven cylindrical container behind the blades was filled with seeds that were dropped into the freshly ploughed ground. This design also helped to weed the ground while quickly and evenly adding cotton seeds.

Henry died in 1860 at the age of 52.

WILLIAM (BILLY) WAYNE BLANKS

Tae Bo Fitness System

William Wayne Blanks is a fitness guru, martial artist and actor who created Tae Bo, a fitness system that combines martial arts and boxing.

William – known as Billy – was born in 1955 in Pennsylvania, US. At the age of 12, he saw martial arts expert and actor Bruce Lee on television and decided he wanted to be a world martial arts champion.

He began studying martial arts (a fighting style used in self-defence or to attack) and attended classes in karate and Taekwondo. He has won seven world karate championships and 36 gold medals in international competitions. In 1980, he was captain of the US Olympic Karate team.

In the late 1980s, Billy developed the Tae Bo fitness system while running a karate studio in Massachusetts, using components of his martial arts and boxing training. The name *Tae bo* is a combination of parts of the words *Tae*kwondo and *bo*xing. He opened a fitness centre in Los Angeles, California, to teach his new fitness system, which attracted celebrity clients when the popularity of his workout grew.

In 1988, Billy was hired as a bodyguard for a lead actress in a film being shot in the Philippines, where he ended up being written into the script in a supporting role. This led to work in other martial arts films and he has appeared in more than 20 Hollywood films.

Billy's unique fitness system became a pop culture phenomenon after he released mass-marketed videos demonstrating the workout. Tae Bo was considered the ultimate total body workout and is reminiscent of the late 1990s.

BESSIE VIRGINIA BLOUNT

Electronic Feeding Device

Bessie Virginia Blount was a nurse, physical therapist, and forensic scientist who invented an electronic feeding device to help injured people feed themselves.

Born in 1914 in Virginia, US, she attended Panzar College of Physical Education in New Jersey and completed her studies in Illinois to become a physical therapist.

Bessie helped soldiers with amputated limbs after World War II (1939-1945) had ended. She taught them to find new ways to perform basic tasks and created an electronic feeding device, which was a neck brace with built-in support for a food container that could be operated by soldiers with lost limbs to feed themselves.

She also invented a kidney-shaped disposable cardboard bowl by moulding and baking a mixture of flour, water, and newspaper. This type of disposable container was used as an emesis or vomit bowl and is still used in hospitals today for medical waste.

In the 1970s, Bessie had a second career, as a forensic scientist. She was a handwriting expert and she helped police solve crimes through scientific techniques and tests to spot forgeries and fake documents. In 1977, she became the first Black woman to train and work at Scotland Yard in the UK. She later started her own business using her forensic training to examine the authenticity of documents from before the American Civil War (1861-1865).

Bessie died in 2009 in New Jersey at the age of 95.

SARAH MARSHALL BOONE

Ironing Board

Sarah Marshall Boone was a dressmaker who invented the ironing board. She was one of the first Black women in the US to receive a patent that helped to improve home technology.

Sarah was born in 1832 in North Carolina, US and later moved to Connecticut, where she worked as a dressmaker.

Her ironing board invention was made from a narrow wooden board with a curved design, collapsible legs, and a padded cover. Before that, ironing was done on a simple plank of wood placed across the back of two chairs.

Sarah's design made it easier to iron clothing, especially sleeves and women's clothes, which were very elaborate in those days. Her invention was patented in 1892, and her design forms the basis for ironing boards used today.

She died in 1904 in Connecticut at the age of 71.

OTIS FRANK BOYKIN

Artificial Heart Pacemaker Control Unit

Otis Frank Boykin was an engineer who invented a control unit for the pacemaker, a device that helps the heart beat properly.

Born in 1920 in Texas, US, he studied at Fisk University in Tennessee while working at the college's aerospace laboratory and graduated in 1941.

Otis worked in electronics and began inventing products on his own. In 1947, he started his own business, Boykin-Fruth Incorporated.

He is best known for inventing electronic control devices. His artificial heart pacemaker control unit uses electrical impulses to control heartbeats, which helps people with slow or irregular heartbeats. It also helps to treat people with heart failure. His mother died from heart failure when he was just one year old so his invention was a personal goal.

Otis had 26 patents to his name. One of his early inventions was a wire precision resistor used in televisions and radios, a breakthrough device that could withstand extreme changes in temperature and pressure. It was cheaper and more reliable than other versions on the market and was in great demand by the US military for guided missiles and by IBM (International Business Machines Corporation) for computers.

He died in 1982 in Illinois at the age of 61.

BENJAMIN BRADLEY

Marine Steam Engine

Benjamin Bradley was a mechanical engineer who invented the marine steam engine for a boat or ship.

He was born in 1836 in Maryland, US, and worked in a printing office from a young age. When Benjamin was 16, he proved his skill in mechanical engineering by making a working model of a steam engine using two pieces of steel, a gun barrel, and pewter.

His natural talent for inventing was noticed by his employer, and he was sent to the Naval Academy in Maryland to work as a classroom assistant in the science department, where he helped to set up lab experiments for teaching staff. He was the first Black person to hold such a post at the Academy, and he impressed the professors with his skills.

Benjamin sold his original steam engine model to one of the students at the academy and was able to buy the materials to build a larger model. At around 1856, he built a steam engine that was able to drive the first sloop-of-war, a warship carrying guns on one of its decks.

He was not able to patent his invention at the time and sold the rights to it instead. His work was recognised and valued by the Naval Academy, and he was later given a teaching position there until he retired.

Benjamin died in 1897 in Massachusetts at the age of 64.

CHARLES BROOKS

Road Sweeper Machine (improvement)

Charles Brooks was a railway porter who designed the road sweeper machine.

He was born in 1865 in Virginia, US. By the 1890s, he was living in New Jersey and working as a porter for a railway company.

In 1893, Charles invented the first paper hole puncher, which was also known as a ticket punch. It had a built-in container to collect the round pieces of waste paper, to prevent littering.

His version of the road sweeper machine was patented in 1896. It had interchangeable revolving brushes attached to the front with scrapers used for clearing snow and ice in the winter. There was a wheel drive for turning the brushes and a lifting mechanism for the scrapers. He added a collecting pan for the swept-up dirt, which was carried along a belt and placed into a container.

Charles's design for the road sweeper machine was very successful and highly praised. It received financial backing, was manufactured and used by cities in the US to help clean their streets, and is still in use today.

He later patented a dustproof bag for use with the road sweeper machine to store the collected dirt. He also included an elastic strap to enable the easy opening and closing of the bag without spilling its contents.

Charles died in 1908 in New Jersey at the age of 43.

HENRY BROWN

Strongbox/Fire Safe

Henry Brown invented a strongbox, a fire- and accident-safe container made of metal that could be sealed with a lock and key for storing and preserving papers.

He was living in Washington, DC, US at the time that he patented his strongbox (or fire safe) in 1886.

Henry's invention was made with a series of hinged trays. When opened, one or more of the trays could be lifted separately to allow for the safe storage of papers.

It was a useful design for storing delicate carbon papers to minimise the risk of damaging documents. At the time, carbon papers were used in typewriters to create copies of documents. These carbon papers were flimsy and could be easily torn or smudged, so they had to be stored carefully.

Henry's impenetrable box allowed for the secure and safe storage of important documents as well as money, jewellery, and other valuable items, whether at home, in the office or factory, or at a bank. It kept them private and helped to reduce the chances of theft.

MARIE VAN BRITTAN BROWN

Home Security System

Marie van Brittan Brown was a nurse who invented the first home security system and an early form of closed-circuit television (CCTV).

She was born in 1922 in New York, US. As a nurse, Marie worked irregular hours, day and night. She lived in an area where the crime rate was very high and so she looked for ways to increase her level of personal security. She decided that she needed a system that would let her know who was at her home and would enable her to contact the police for help as quickly as possible.

This led her to invent the first home security system with the assistance of her husband, Albert Brown, an electronics technician who also worked irregular hours.

Her invention was made of peepholes in the front door at different heights to see who was outside, a sliding camera that could stop at any one of four points to record images that were projected onto a television monitor, a two-way microphone to speak to someone outside without having to open the front door, an alarm button to contact the police immediately, and a remote control to unlock the front door. Marie received a patent for her home security system in 1969.

She died in 1999 in New York at the age of 76.

OSCAR BROWN

Horseshoe (improvement)

Oscar Brown was an inventor who created an improved horseshoe.

Born in 1871 in Iowa, US, Oscar's horseshoe invention was patented in 1892 in New York.

At that time, people normally used horses to travel everywhere. Horseshoes protect horses by preventing their hooves from wearing down. They are nailed into the hooves to prevent soreness after long walks on hard ground.

Oscar created a double- or compound-horseshoe. Before that, horseshoes did not fit well on horses' hooves. His horseshoe was made of an upper shoe that was fixed to the hoof and a lower shoe that could be easily removed and replaced. The main part of this invention was a lock mechanism that helped to fit the lower shoe to the upper shoe, and the horse experienced less discomfort when only the lower shoe needed to be removed.

Modern horseshoes are similar to his design as both are made of metal, and they have the same parts.

Oscar died in 1960 in Missouri at the age of 89.

JOHN ALBERT BURR

Lawnmower (improvement)

John Albert Burr was a mechanical engineer who made improvements to the lawnmower.

He was born in 1848 in Maryland, US. As a teenager, John worked as a farm labourer where his mechanical skills were recognised, and he was given the opportunity to attend engineering classes at a private university.

He put his skills to good use and made a living repairing and maintaining farm equipment and other machines. He moved to Illinois, where he worked as a steelworker and later moved to Massachusetts.

In 1899, John patented a lawnmower with traction wheels and a rotary blade that prevented the machine from becoming clogged with lawn clippings. He improved the lawnmower further by making it possible to mow closer to the edges of buildings and walls. His lawnmower design is similar to the ones used today.

He also designed devices for mulching lawn clippings, which returns nutrients to the ground rather than disposing of them. His inventions helped to save labour and were also good for the grass and ground.

John held over 30 patents for lawn care and agricultural inventions. He enjoyed the fruits of his success, receiving payments for his creations, which allowed him to travel and hold lectures later in life.

He died in 1926 in Pennsylvania at the age of 78.

GEORGE ROBERT CARRUTHERS

Ultraviolet Camera/Spectrograph

Dr George Robert Carruthers was a physicist who invented the ultraviolet (UV) camera (or spectrograph) to help us learn more about the Earth and the universe.

George was born in 1939 in Ohio, US. He was an inventive and inquisitive child who built his first telescope at the age of ten and won awards at school science fairs where few Black children were represented.

He attended the University of Illinois where he earned his bachelor's degree in physics, master's degree in nuclear engineering, and a postgraduate degree in aeronautical and astronautical engineering.

George worked at the US Naval Research Laboratory in Washington, DC, where he led the team that invented the ultraviolet camera or spectrograph, which was used for the Apollo 16 space mission to the moon in 1972. An ultraviolet camera is designed to show images in the ultraviolet part of the electromagnetic spectrum (the range of all types of radiation, which is energy that travels and spreads out as it goes) that we normally cannot see. This meant that, for the first time, scientists were able to examine the Earth's atmosphere for concentrations of pollutants and see ultraviolet images of more than 550 stars, nebulae (clouds of dust and gases among the stars), and galaxies.

In the 1980s, one of George's inventions captured an ultraviolet image of Halley's Comet, the famous comet that comes close to the Earth around every 75 years. In 1991, he invented an instrument with two cameras that had different ultraviolet wavelength sensitivities which was used in the Space Transportation System STS-39 Space Shuttle Discovery mission.

He received many awards, including NASA's Exceptional Scientific Achievement Medal and the US National Medal for Technology and Innovation awarded by President Barack Obama.

George died in 2020 in Washington, DC at the age of 81.

GEORGE WASHINGTON CARVER

Peanut Products

George Washington Carver was a botanist and teacher who devised over 300 different uses for peanuts, including cooking oil, ink, dyes, plastics, milk, paints, cosmetics, medicinal oils, soap, wood stains, axle grease, and gasoline.

George was born in 1864 in Missouri, US. He was interested in both the sciences and the arts and studied agricultural science, botanical studies, art, and music in Iowa.

He was the first Black student at Iowa State Agricultural College. After graduating in 1896, he was hired by Booker T Washington, the famous founder of the historically Black Tuskegee Institute in Alabama, to run the school's agricultural department. Historically Black Colleges and Universities (HBCU) were originally established to serve the educational needs of Black people who were previously excluded from this education.

George established a reputation as a brilliant botanist. His areas of research and training included methods for crop rotation and the development of alternative cash crops, including peanuts and sweet potatoes.

He became a prominent scientific expert both nationally and internationally and one of the most famous Black Americans of his time. US President Theodore Roosevelt sought his advice on agricultural matters, and George also advised Indian leader Mahatma Gandhi on matters of agriculture and nutrition.

The first national monument dedicated to a Black person in the US was built in his honour. He has appeared on US commemorative postal stamps and coins, and many schools and two US military vessels were named after him.

George died in 1943 in Alabama at the age of 78.

ALFRED CRALLE

Ice Cream Scoop

Alfred Cralle was a businessman who invented the ice cream scoop, originally known as the ice cream moulder and disher.

He was born in 1866 in Virginia, US and showed an early interest in how things worked. As a young man, Alfred worked with his father in the carpentry trade. He developed an interest in mechanics and was sent to attend Wayland Seminary in Washington, DC, an institute that educated Black men after the American Civil War (1861-1865).

After completing his education, he moved to Pennsylvania where he worked as a porter at a pharmacy. He went on to work at a hotel where he devised the idea for his invention when he noticed the difficulty servers had trying to scoop ice cream with spoons and ladles using two hands. His ice cream mould and disher had a built-in scraper to allow for one-handed operation, and this is how ice cream scoops are made today.

Alfred's invention was patented in 1897. It was strong, effective, and inexpensive and allowed ice cream to be served faster and more hygienically.

He became a successful business promoter and when local Black investors formed the Afro-American Financial, Accumulating, Merchandise, and Business Association, he was selected as a one of the managers.

Alfred died in 1919 in Pennsylvania at the age of 53.

MARIAN ROGERS CROAK

Voice Over Internet Protocol (VOIP)

Dr Marian Rogers Croak is an engineer and technology leader who created the Voice Over Internet Protocol (VOIP) technology.

Marian was born in 1955 in Pennsylvania, US. She holds a postgraduate degree in qualitative analysis and social psychology from Princeton University in New Jersey.

She joined Bell Laboratories, a large research company that develops a wide range of new technologies, where she worked in voice and data communication. She holds over 200 patents, most of them in Voice Over Internet Protocol (VOIP), which allows for the delivery of voice communications and multimedia sessions over Internet Protocol (IP) networks. This has helped to advance the technology used in mobile phones.

Marian also pioneered the use of phone network services to make it easier for people to donate to crisis appeals, which revolutionised the donation of money to charitable organisations.

In 2013, she was inducted into the Women in Technology International Hall of Fame. In 2014, she received the Black Engineer of the Year Award and was voted 'Most Influential Woman in Wireless' by FierceWireless.

In 2014, Marian started working for Google as their vice president for engineering, where she was responsible for getting the Internet into all areas of the world and for engineering many of Google's services for increased reliability.

MICHAEL CROSLIN

Computerised Blood Pressure and Pulse Monitor

Dr Michael Croslin is a biomedical engineer who invented a computerised digital blood pressure and pulse monitor.

He was born in 1933 in St Croix, US Virgin Islands in the Caribbean. Originally named Miguel, he was abandoned as a baby. By the time he was 12 years old, he had fled the Islands for mainland US, where he worked odd jobs while living in Georgia. He ended up in Wisconsin, where he was adopted by the Croslin family, and his name was changed to Michael Croslin.

Despite his unsettled childhood and education, he was a brilliant student. By the age of 14, he had finished high school, and three years later he had completed a bachelor's of science degree at the University of Wisconsin.

Michael joined the US Air Force in 1950, serving in Korea and Vietnam. On his return, he went on to study further and earned a second bachelor's degree in mechanical engineering, a master's degree in electrical engineering in 1963, and a postgraduate degree in biomedical engineering in 1968 at New York University. At the same time, he earned a master's degree in business administration at Columbia University in New York.

As a biomedical engineer, Michael designed, developed, and maintained equipment used for diagnosing illnesses and treating patients. He invented the Medtek 410 computerised blood pressure and pulse monitor in 1978, and established his own company, Medtek Corporation, to produce and distribute his inventions. The Medtek 410 took the guesswork out of monitoring a patient's vital signs (the body's most basic functions: body temperature, pulse rate, respiration rate, and blood pressure), allowing medical professionals to diagnose and treat patients.

A later model of his blood pressure and pulse monitor, the Medtek 420, adjusted for air pressure and surrounding noise. The Medtek 420 was used in emergency medical evacuation helicopters, transporting seriousy ill patients from one hospital to another for urgent treatment by specialists.

Michael holds more than 40 patents for medical inventions.

WILLIAM DAVIS

Riding Saddle (improvement)

William Davis was a Buffalo Soldier who invented an improved riding saddle for horses.

He was based at Fort Assinniboine in Montana, US, when he patented his riding saddle in 1896.

William joined the US Army following the American Civil War (1861-1865) at a time when Black men were only allowed to serve in the all-Black 9th and 10th Cavalry and 24th and 25th Infantry Regiments formed in 1866. They were based in forts – military buildings designed to be strongly protected from attack – throughout the mountainous state of Montana, and became famously known as Buffalo Soldiers due to their bravery and stamina in battle.

The Buffalo Soldiers' main tasks were to guard the vast borders of the Western frontier, capture cattle rustlers and thieves, and protect settlers, stagecoaches, wagon trains, railway crews, and the US mail. These soldiers were extremely skilled horsemen, known for taking long journeys on difficult terrain while travelling by horse, which was not a comfortable experience.

This led to William's improvement to the riding saddle. He added springs beneath the seat and at the tops of the stirrups, which provided a smoother ride for soldiers, cowboys, and other horse riders.

MARK DEAN

Personal Computer Technology

Dr Mark Dean is a computer scientist and engineer who co-invented the IBM (International Business Machines Corporation) personal computer.

Mark was born in 1957 in Tennessee, US. He loved to build things from an early age. As a young boy, he built a tractor with his father from scratch.

He was also a gifted athlete and an extremely smart student who graduated at the top of his class at the University of Tennessee, where he earned his bachelor's degree in engineering. He earned his master's degree in electrical engineering at Florida's Atlantic University and his doctorate in electrical engineering at Stanford University in California.

Mark began working for IBM in the 1980s and co-invented, with Dennis Moeller, a new technology that allowed support devices – such as disk drives, printers, monitors and mice – to be connected to a computer. They called this the Industry Standard Architecture (ISA) systems bus.

He also developed the colour monitor for personal computers and, in 1999, he led the team that developed the first gigahertz computer processor chip (which provides the instructions and power a computer needs to do its work), allowing for faster calculations and speed in personal computers.

In 1996, Mark was named an IBM Fellow, the first Black person to receive the honour. In 1997, he was honoured with the Black Engineer of the Year President's Award.

MARY JONES DE LEON

Cooking Apparatus/Steam Table

Mary Jones De Leon invented a cooking apparatus which was an early version of the steam table. She was one of the first Black women in the US to receive a patent for an invention.

Mary was living in Maryland, US, at the time of her patent in 1873.

Her cooking apparatus invention consisted of the construction and arrangement of a device that heated or cooked food using dry heat and steam at the same time. It included a lamp and a water reservoir with perforations to allow steam to escape into a perforated tray where food was placed for heating. The lamp heated the water in the reservoir to generate steam and also heated the underside of the food tray by a series of tubes. Her apparatus combined the functions of an oven and a steamer which saved space and energy.

Mary's invention was an early design for the steam tables we see at food buffets in restaurants and venues all around the world today, to help keep food warm during large gatherings when food is served at different times.

PHILIP BELL DOWNING

Post Box

Philip Bell Downing was an inventor who designed the street post box, to shelter mail from all types of weather.

He was born in 1857 in Rhode Island, US, and was living in Massachusetts when he successfully filed at least five patents during his lifetime. His family were prominent and successful business owners.

In 1890, Philip received a patent for a railway electrical switch, which allowed train drivers to turn the power supply on and off for trains as and when this was needed. Today, electrical switches such as light switches are based on this design.

His most significant invention was the post box, which was patented in 1891. His design resembled street letter boxes found everywhere in the US today – a tall, metal box with a secure, hinged door through which letters were dropped for posting. Before that, people had to go to the post office to send mail. Philip's invention allowed people to drop off mail closer to their homes, which would then be picked up by postmen. The hinged opening prevented rain or snow from entering the box and damaging the mail.

In 1917, he received a patent for an envelope moistener, which used a roller and a small, attached water tank to moisten envelopes so they could be sealed. In 1918, he patented a new type of desktop notepad.

Philip died in 1934 in Massachusetts at the age of 77.

CHARLES RICHARD DREW

Blood Bank

Dr Charles Richard Drew was a surgeon and medical researcher who pioneered methods for storing blood plasma for blood transfusions.

Charles was born in 1904 in Washington, DC, US. He was a very talented athlete, but he also wanted to study medicine. He attended medical school at McGill University in Canada, and graduated in 1933 with both doctor of medicine and master of surgery degrees.

He did his internship and residency in Canada, where he examined problems and issues regarding blood transfusions. Returning to the US, he studied at Columbia University in New York while continuing his exploration of blood-related matters. He was the first Black person to receive a doctorate from Columbia University in 1940.

Charles developed a method of processing and preserving blood plasma, which lasts much longer than whole blood and makes it possible to store for long periods of time. Blood plasma is the fluid that carries blood components – white blood cells, red blood cells, and platelets – throughout the body. His invention allowed the plasma to be dried for easier storage and rehydrated, returning it to its original form when needed.

During World War II (1939-1945), he managed two of the largest blood banks for the US and the UK. In 1941, he led a blood bank effort for the American Red Cross and the National Blood Donor Service and was known as the 'Father of blood banking.' He initiated the use of mobile blood donation trucks ('bloodmobiles') and blood donation stations with refrigerators to store the blood. He also became the first Black examiner for the American Board of Surgery in 1941.

Charles died in 1950 in Alabama at the age of 45.

ELLEN EGLIN

Clothes Wringer

Ellen Eglin was a housekeeper who invented the clothes wringer.

She was born in 1849 in Washington, DC, US, and worked as a housekeeper at a time when doing laundry was a dreaded chore. Fuel and water had to be gathered, clothes had to be scrubbed and wrung out by hand, hung to dry, and then pressed with heavy irons heated on a stove.

To help make this process easier, Ellen created her clothes wringer. It was made of two rollers in a frame connected to a crank handle to turn the rollers. Wet clothes were fed between the two rollers, and water was pressed out of the material as the crank handle was turned, which helped the laundry to dry faster.

Ellen was concerned that people would not buy her invention because she was Black, so she sold it in 1888.

Her invention brought its new owner great financial success, and her wringer design is still used today in everyday products such as mop buckets and wringers where the same principle applies.

THOMAS ELKINS

Refrigeration Apparatus

Dr Thomas Elkins was a pharmacist who designed a refrigeration apparatus.

He was born in 1818 in New York, US, and studied surgery and dentistry with one of the founders of the Albany Medical College in New York.

Thomas managed a pharmacy that offered dental services. He was also a district doctor and inventor who designed many items for everyday use.

In 1870, he patented a combined dining table, ironing table and quilting frame, which was effectively a multi-purpose folding table. In 1872, he patented a chamber commode. This piece of furniture was a combined desk, chair, bookshelf, mirror, washbasin, table, and chamber stool with a pot under it for use as a toilet, which was common in those days. His invention formed the basis for modern bathrooms today.

Thomas carried out important work in the development of refrigeration techniques. He designed a refrigerator to help preserve fresh foods through a method of chilling using the evaporation of water, which he patented in 1879 as a refrigeration apparatus.

During the American Civil War (1861-1865), he served as a medical examiner, where he investigated and determined causes of deaths. His refrigeration technique helped to preserve the bodies using a device that included a covered trough or container kept at a low temperature by the continuous circulation of chilled water or other cooling fluid through a series of metallic coils.

Thomas died in 1900 in New York at the age of 82.

PHILIP EMEAGWALI

Supercomputer

Dr Philip Emeagwali is a computer scientist who invented the world's fastest computer. He is known as the 'Bill Gates of Africa' and the 'Father of the Internet.'

Philip was born in 1954 in Nigeria. He was forced to leave school at the age of 13 due to the Nigerian Civil War (1967-1970) when he was drafted into the Biafran Armed Forces.

After the war, his father taught him at home, where he performed mental exercises, such as solving 100 maths problems an hour every day. He was considered a maths prodigy and received a scholarship to study in the US, where he received a bachelor's degree in mathematics from Oregon State University in 1977.

Philip holds a master's degree in ocean and marine engineering from George Washington University in Washington, DC, and a second master's degree in applied mathematics from the University of Maryland. He received a postgraduate degree in scientific computing from the University of Michigan.

He also studied nature, and specifically bees. The construction of the honeycomb by bees inspired him to apply the same process to computers. In 1989, his idea helped him create the world's fastest supercomputer, using 65,000 computers to perform 3.1 billion calculations per second, linked in parallel to form what was called the Connection Machine. This was a practical and inexpensive way to allow computers all around the world to speak with each other and work better together.

The key to his achievement was programming each computer to talk with six other neighbouring computers at the same time. This discovery led to the development of the Internet. Philip also designed the Hyperball computer, to forecast long-term global warming patterns.

Among his many awards, he also won the Association for Computing Machinery Gordon Bell Prize for contributions to computer science and the world community in 1989.

ROBERT FRANCIS FLEMMING JR

Acoustic Guitar (modern)

Robert Francis Flemming Jr was a musician, composer, and music store owner who invented the acoustic guitar.

Born in 1839 in Maryland, US, Robert joined the US Navy during the American Civil War (1861-1865) where he witnessed the sinking of some historical ships and was involved in a few battles.

After the war, he settled in Massachusetts and opened a music store where he gave music lessons and built guitars.

Although string instruments had existed in Africa for many years before this period, Robert's guitar had a more resonant sound and looked different. It was designed to produce a louder sound with less force required than traditional string instruments. He called his guitar a Euphonica and patented it in the US in 1886, and in Canada in 1887. Modern acoustic guitars today are based on his design.

Robert died in 1919 in Massachusetts at the age of 79.

LISA GELOBTER

Web Animation Technology

Lisa Gelobter is a computer scientist and entrepreneur who developed the technology that formed the beginning of web animation.

She was born in 1971 in the US and is a graduate of Brown University in Rhode Island with a bachelor's degree in computer science, specialising in artificial intelligence and machine learning.

Lisa worked in computer software and digital technology and was involved in the early stages of several pioneering Internet technologies. She developed the web animation technology used to create Graphics Interchange Format (GIF) images.

She was also involved in the development of video on the Internet through online video companies Brightcove, Joost and TheFeedRoom, and was on the senior management team at Hulu, a subscription video-on-demand service controlled by the Walt Disney Company.

Lisa worked for the Black Entertainment Television (BET) Network, where she ran the technology, product, and business operations departments. She also worked at the White House in the Department of Education's digital service during Barack Obama's presidency.

In 2016, she co-founded tEQuitable, a platform that helps to ensure good practices in the workplace.

SARAH ELISABETH JACOBS GOODE

Folding Cabinet Bed

Sarah Elisabeth Jacobs Goode was an entrepreneur who invented a folding cabinet bed. She was one of the first Black women to receive a US patent for her invention.

Sarah was born in 1855 in Ohio, US. After the American Civil War (1861-1865), she moved with her family to Illinois. She was an entrepreneur who owned a furniture store, and that was where she invented her revolutionary bed design, for which she received a patent in 1885.

Many customers at Sarah's furniture store were working-class people who lived in small apartments where there was little space for furniture, including beds. As a solution, she invented the folding cabinet bed. When the bed was not being used, it could be folded up and used as a desk, which had various compartments for stationery and other writing materials.

Her invention is similar to what is now called a Murphy bed, which is a pull-down or fold-down bed. It is hinged at one end to store vertically against a wall or inside a cupboard when not in use, and it saves space in a small room or home.

Sarah died in 1905 in Illinois at the age of 50.

MEREDITH CHARLES GOURDINE

Electrostatic Precipitator Filtration System

Dr Meredith Charles Gourdine was a physicist and engineer who invented the electrostatic precipitator filtration system, which removes fine particles from the air.

Meredith, also known as 'Flash' due to his sporting abilities, was born in 1929 in New York, US. He was a star athlete in swimming, running, jumping, and throwing sports. While studying for his bachelor's degree in engineering physics at Cornell University in New York, he also won many sports championship titles and became a silver medalist in the long jump at the 1952 Olympics in Helsinki, Finland.

In 1953, he joined the US Navy as an officer before going on to study at the California Institute of Technology, where he earned a doctorate in engineering physics in 1960.

After initially working in private industry, Meredith opened his own research and development company in New Jersey in 1964, called Gourdine Systems. In 1973, he founded another company, Energy Innovations, in Houston, Texas.

He was an expert in electrogasdynamics, a process that creates electrical energy. His companies received patents for converting natural gas to electricity; for desalinating seawater, which is the removal of salts and minerals from seawater to make fresh water to use in agriculture and industry; for creating circuit breakers, which interrupt the flow of electricity when a fault is detected; and for acoustic imaging, which uses ultrasound to produce images to see through solid internal structures. He also invented the focus flow heat sink, which cools computer chips to stop them from overheating.

From 1971 to 1973, Meredith received patents for various electrostatic precipitator filtration systems that clear the air by introducing a negative charge to airborne particles, which are then electromagnetically attracted to the ground and so they drop down and fresh air fills their original space. His engineering technique, called 'Incineraid', helps to remove smoke from burning buildings. In 1987, he patented a method of removing fog from airport runways. His invention also helps to remove allergens and other particles from the air in homes and other buildings.

He died in 1998 in Houston at the age of 69.

GEORGE FRANKLIN GRANT

Oblate Palate

Dr George Franklin Grant was a dentist who invented the oblate palate, a prosthetic device worn by patients who were born with cleft palates (where the bones and soft tissue in the roof of the mouth have not closed properly).

George was born in 1846 in New York, US. When he was 15 years old, he was hired by a dentist as an errand boy. He soon became a lab assistant and was encouraged to pursue a career in dentistry.

He was one of the first Black men to graduate from the Harvard School of Dental Medicine in Massachusetts, and in 1870, he became the first Black faculty member at Harvard University.

George was the founding member and president of the Harvard Odonatological Society, and in 1881, he was elected president of the Harvard Dental Association. He was a very successful dentist who specialised in treating patients with cleft palates. He invented the oblate palate, which was patented in 1889, to help the cleft palates line up so that patients could speak and eat more normally.

He was a keen golfer, and this led to another famous invention of his in 1899. He created the golf tee – a small stand used to elevate a golf ball before striking it with a golf club – by designing a wooden peg topped with gutta-percha, a rubbery substance from the percha tree, used by dentists in root canal work. Before that, golfers would have to create a little mound of soil on the ground to act as a golf tee, which was tedious and messy.

George died in 1910 in New Hampshire at the age of 63.

LLOYD AUGUSTUS HALL

Food Preservatives

Dr Lloyd Augustus Hall was a chemist who is best known for his work on food preservation techniques to slow down or stop food spoilage.

Lloyd was born in 1894 in Illinois, US. He earned his bachelor's and master's degrees in pharmaceutical chemistry at Northwestern University in Illinois, and his postgraduate degree in science at Virginia State College.

He worked as a chemist at various organisations where he invented a few different ways to preserve food. His methods helped to pioneer many food preservatives used today. In 1932, he invented his process for curing or preserving meat using sodium chloride, nitrate, and nitrite crystals, which are chemicals he combined to stop the nitrogen that spoils meat. This process was known as flash-drying and is still used today to cure meats.

Lloyd developed antioxidants, which stop food fats and oils from spoiling when they react with oxygen. He also discovered that some spices exposed food to microbes (tiny living organisms which cannot be seen but are everywhere, and some of them make people sick) that speed up the process of food spoilage. He created a system to sterilise spices by using ethylene gas in a vacuum chamber to destroy the microbes. This system was later adapted by the food, pharmaceutical, and cosmetic industries to help preserve their products.

He became a consultant for the Food and Agriculture Organisation of the United Nations (UN) and was responsible for formulating many meat curing products, seasonings, baking products, antioxidants, and other substances that keep food fresh and flavourful. His scientific contributions made him one of the top food chemists at the time.

During World War I (1914-1918), Lloyd worked on powerful explosives for the US government, and was a consultant in the US Army's agricultural development and research laboratories during World War II (1939-1945). He held over 100 patents in the US, the UK, and Canada.

He died in 1971 in California at the age of 76.

JOANNA NAYER HARDIN

CompUrest Keyboard Stand

Joanna Nayer Hardin is an entrepreneur who co-invented the CompUrest keyboard stand.

She was born in 1952 in New York, US, learnt to type in 1966, and regularly used a keyboard for her work. By the 1980s, Joanna had osteoarthritis pain from stiff joints in her neck, back, and limbs, due to repetitive movement from using a computer and keyboard for long periods of time.

While watching her grandmother resting her arms on elevated pillows after long days at work, cleaning houses and styling hair, she came up with an idea. With the help of her friend Bernie Hirschenson, she designed a device to support the arms, elbows, shoulders, and fingers, hands, and wrists while using a keyboard. It also helped with better posture. When she tested the device herself, her symptoms disappeared within a month. They called their invention the CompUrest keyboard stand, which was patented in 1991.

In 1994, Joanna founded Computer Underground Railroad Enterprises, a community business with computer-related activities. She became known as 'The Computer Lady', or Harlem's 'Computer Diva'.

She created a style of computer training called 'How To Compute' that helped people learn how to use a personal computer, and increased computer literacy in her area. Her training and classes were featured on television shows in New York in the 1990s.

With Peter Segall, Joanna also co-invented an envelope for a floppy disk that allowed the disk's directory to be printed on it, to help label a disk with its contents.

BETTY WRIGHT HARRIS

Explosives Spot Test

Dr Betty Wright Harris is an organic analytical chemist who invented a spot test to detect triaminotrinitrobenzene (TATB), a powerful explosive.

Betty was born in 1940 in Louisiana, US. She earned her bachelor's degree in chemistry at Southern University in Louisiana in 1961, and her master's degree in chemistry at Atlanta University in Georgia in 1963. She earned her postgraduate degree in chemistry at the University of New Mexico in 1973.

She started work as an assistant university professor of chemistry and mathematics and went on to work at Los Alamos National Laboratory, a large science and technology company, where she became a leading expert on explosives and nuclear weapons. She is also an expert on the clean-up of hazardous and dangerous materials and on restoring damaged environments.

As an organic analytical chemist, Betty experimented with chemicals to develop and make new, useful products. In 1986, she patented a simple and extremely sensitive spot test for the presence of TATB, which allowed the military and private industries to quickly locate explosive materials and safely remove them.

Betty encouraged young Black girls in the Girl Scouts to study chemistry and developed their badge for chemistry. She is recognised for revolutionising the world of chemistry and is a member of the American Chemical Society and the American Society for the Advancement of Science. In 1999, she received an award for Outstanding New Mexico Women.

MICHAEL HARVEY

Lantern (improvement)

Michael Harvey (sometimes written as Harney) was an inventor
known for improving the lantern, an important source of light
at the time.

Michael was born in 1854 in Missouri, US.

During his time, lanterns were used by miners working underground because they were easily portable and could be turned on and off, allowing miners to send signals to each other as a means of communication. This was important as they worked in dangerous situations underground and needed to be able to warn each other of any danger, such as tunnel collapses, explosions, toxic air and flooding.

Michael invented an improvement in the wick-raiser running through a lantern, allowing it to burn by capillary action, which pulled liquid fuel up the wick rope to keep the flame burning at the top of the wick. This made the lantern more efficient. He received a patent for his invention in 1884.

WALTER LINCOLN HAWKINS

Plastic Cable Coating

Dr Walter Lincoln Hawkins was a chemist and engineer who invented a plastic cable coating that wraps around and protects telecommunications wires.

Walter was born in 1911 in Washington, DC, US. He was orphaned as a young child and raised by his sister. He enjoyed maths and science and received a bachelor's degree in chemical engineering from Rensselaer Polytechnic Institute in New York, a master's degree in chemistry from Howard University in Washington, DC, and a doctorate in chemistry from McGill University in Canada.

He was the first Black scientist to work at Bell Laboratories, a large research company that develops a wide range of new technologies, where he gained a reputation for extending the life of plastics. He also conducted research on polymers (natural or synthetic materials, including plastics) for telecommunications (the exchange of information over a distance, such as by telephone).

Up until around 1950, telephone cables had been coated with an expensive and toxic lead-based material, which was later replaced by polyethylene. These early plastic coatings became brittle quickly and were breakable in sunlight.

In 1956, Walter invented a polymer which was essentially a plastic containing a chemical additive composed of carbon and antioxidants that prevented the material from deteriorating under a range of conditions. His plastic cable coating became widely used as an inexpensive, durable, and safe coating for telecommunications wire and it is still used today.

Walter also contributed to the development of techniques for recycling and reusing plastics. He was an educator and industrial visionary who received many awards for his work.

He died in 1992 in California at the age of 81.

RONALD (RON) GEORGE ALPHONSO HEADLEY

Ecocharger/Car Engine Emission System

Ronald George Alphonso Headley is a former West Indies cricket player and businessman who invented the Ecocharger car engine emission system, which improved the performance of diesel cars.

Ronald, known as Ron, was born in 1939 in Jamaica in the Caribbean. He moved to England at the age of 13. Like his father, George Headley MBE (Member of the Most Excellent Order of the British Empire), he played cricket internationally for the West indies before moving on to work in the car industry.

Ron invented the Ecocharger, which reduces smoke emission, car pollution, and fuel consumption, and allows cars to run for 150,000 miles without major maintenance.

He spent 20 years developing his Ecocharger, which works on fuel before combustion. As the fuel reaches the engine, the Ecocharger makes the size of the fuel droplets much smaller, which increases the efficiency of combustion. This means there is less unburnt fuel and waste sent out through the exhaust system, so there is no need for a catalytic converter to clean up the waste further down the exhaust system.

Ron patented his revolutionary invention in 1985. The Ecocharger is customised for the specifications of each car's engine and his diesel engine emission system helps to clean up the air.

ASKWAR HILONGA

Sand-based Water Filter

Dr Askwar Hilonga is a chemical engineer who invented a sand-based water filter using nanotechnology (the science of working with something at a microscopic level in order to create something useful).

Askwar was born in 1976 in Tanzania. He holds a postgraduate degree in nanotechnology from Hanyang University in South Korea and a doctorate in chemical engineering. He also studied public health and has written numerous papers on these subjects.

Tanzania faces severe water shortages, and although it borders three of Africa's Great Lakes (Lake Victoria, Lake Tanganyika, and Lake Malawi), almost half of its population is based in remote rural areas and cannot access safe drinking water. Surface water and groundwater sources are often contaminated with toxic heavy metals, bacteria, viruses, other pollutants from mining and industrial waste, and poor sewage systems.

Askwar developed a low-cost, customisable water filtration system to clean the water, which has transformed the lives of many Africans. He co-founded Gongali Model, a company that manufactures water filters. His sand-based water filter absorbs everything from copper and fluoride to bacteria, viruses, and pesticides.

It can be customised for a specific individual, or household, or for commercial use. For the filter to work well, he set up the nanoparticles in a way to suit different areas and issues. His filter has been used by businesses, community centres, and local schools to provide clean and cheap drinking water.

Askwar's invention won the Africa Prize for Engineering Innovation from the UK's Royal Academy of Engineering in 2015. He received the President of Tanzania's National Health Innovation Award in 2016.

CHRISTINA MAE THOMAS JENKINS

Hair Weaving and Extensions

Christina Mae Thomas Jenkins was a cosmetologist who created the hair weaving and extensions process.

Born in 1920 in Louisiana, US, Christina graduated from Leland College with a degree in science in 1943. As a cosmetologist she worked in the beauty industry and created hair and beauty products. She moved to Illinois and worked at a wig manufacturer, where she developed a technique to make wigs fit more securely in 1949.

Christina moved again, to Ohio, and began researching how to sew commercial hair to a person's natural hair to add length and body. She developed a hair weaving method designed to make hairstyles longer and fuller by weaving extensions into existing hair. In 1952, she received a patent for her hair weaving method, called the 'HairWeev' technique, which added extensions onto cornrows, where existing hair is braided close to the scalp.

She opened her hairdresser and beauty business, Christina's HairWeev Penthouse Salon, in Ohio to create hairstyles with her invention. She also taught her hair weaving techniques at hair shows throughout Europe, and this method continues to be used by hairstylists today.

She is credited with making a revolutionary contribution, and change, to the field of cosmetology, helping to boost the self-esteem of women and men all around the world.

Christina died in 2003 in Ohio at the age of 82.

THOMAS JENNINGS

Dry Cleaning

Thomas Jennings was a tailor who invented a dry cleaning process called 'dry scouring.' He is known as the first Black person to be granted a patent for his invention.

Born in 1791 in New York, US, Thomas apprenticed as a tailor when he was young and later opened one of New York's leading clothing shops.

Customers often asked him for cleaning advice for their clothes, which inspired him to research and experiment with different solutions and cleaning agents. He tested them on different types of fabrics until he found the right combination to treat and clean each type of material. Thomas called his method of cleaning 'dry scouring', a process now known as dry cleaning. It was patented in 1821 and is essentially the same method used by dry cleaning businesses worldwide today.

Due to his success and wealth, Thomas was highly respected in his community. He became a leader of the civil rights movement and helped to challenge discrimination and segregation in America.

He died in 1859 in New York at the age of 68.

ISAAC JOHNSON

Folding Bicycle Frame

Isaac Johnson was an inventor who designed the folding bicycle frame.

He was born in 1812 in New York, US.

Isaac's folding bicycle frame invention was patented in 1899. His bicycle frame could be folded or taken apart and placed in a vehicle for easier transportation. It could also be placed in a small area to allow for easier storage. The folding bicycle frame was ideal for trips and holidays as it could be easily packed away, transported, and used when needed.

His invention looked similar to the bicycles people ride today.

LONNIE GEORGE JOHNSON

Nerf Water Gun

Lonnie George Johnson is an engineer and entrepreneur who invented a popular water gun, which became a top-selling toy by the early 1990s.

Lonnie was born in 1949 in Alabama, US. His father taught him how to build his own toys, and he dreamt of becoming a famous inventor. He was curious about the way things worked and ambitious in his experimentation; he considers a robot he built in school as one of his best inventions.

He received a bachelor's degree in mechanical engineering, a master's degree in nuclear engineering, and an honorary doctorate in science from Tuskegee University in Alabama.

Lonnie was an engineer for the US Air Force and NASA (National Aeronautics and Space Administration). During his time at NASA, he worked on the Galileo mission to Jupiter, the Mars Observer project, and the Cassini mission to Saturn. He received multiple awards from NASA for his spacecraft control systems.

He worked on his own inventions in his spare time and is one of the most successful inventors and entrepreneurs of his generation, holding more than 250 patents. The inspiration for his water gun came to him while he was working on an eco-friendly heat pump. It is still ranked as a top 20 best-selling toy and was first called the Power Drencher, then the Super Soaker, and is now the Nerf range of water and dart guns. The success of his water gun invention allowed him to work for himself.

In 1991, Lonnie founded the Johnson Research and Development Company, a scientific facility in Georgia researching green technology to create products that are environmentally friendly. One of these is an all-ceramic battery, which uses glass as an electrolyte instead of liquid and holds more charge than a lithium-ion battery. Another product is the Johnson Thermo-electrochemical Converter, an efficient engine that uses hydrogen to convert heat directly into electricity.

Lonnie has also founded two further technology development companies, Excellatron Solid State and Johnson Electro-Mechanical Systems, as well as Johnson Real Estate Investments.

FREDERICK McKINLEY JONES

Portable Refrigeration Unit

Frederick McKinley Jones was an engineer who invented portable refrigeration units for vans carrying perishable food.

Born in 1893 in Ohio, US, Frederick was abandoned at a young age and fended for himself from the age of 11. He received little schooling and taught himself mechanical and electrical engineering, inventing a range of devices while working at a variety of odd jobs. He served in the US Army during World War I (1914-1918).

After the war, he educated himself further in electronics and built a transmitter for a new radio station in his town. He also developed a device to combine motion pictures with sound, the beginnings of modern filmmaking.

Frederick designed and patented a portable refrigeration unit in the 1930s. In 1938, he co-founded the US Thermo Control Company with Joseph Numero, which later became known as Thermo King due to its success. During World War II (1939-1945) the company's air-conditioned vans transported fresh food, blood, and medicine for the US military forces.

He received more than 60 patents throughout his life. Most of these patents related to refrigeration technologies, and the others related to X-ray machines, engines, and sound equipment. In 1944, Frederick became the first Black person to be elected to the American Society of Refrigeration Engineers.

He died in 1961 in Minnesota at the age of 67. In 1991, he was posthumously awarded the National Medal of Technology and was the first Black person to receive this award.

MARJORIE STEWART JOYNER

Permanent Hair Wave Machine

Marjorie Stewart Joyner was a cosmetologist who invented the permanent hair wave machine.

She was born in 1896 in Virginia, US. Marjorie studied cosmetology in Illinois, becoming the first Black person to graduate from the AB Moler Beauty School in 1916.

She opened a beauty salon in Illinois where she met Madam CJ Walker (see contents page), a well-known Black entrepreneur who had invented the Walker hair care system and opened beauty schools around the country. Marjorie joined the Madam CJ Walker Beauty Colleges as their national supervisor and oversaw more than 200 beauty schools.

Before her invention, women curled their hair using very hot curling irons, which was a slow and uncomfortable process as only one iron could be used at a time. In 1928, she created and patented the permanent hair wave machine, which was a new way to curl hair that lasted for days. The invention was inspired by the rods she used when making a pot roast, which heated the meat from the inside out. Marjorie's invention consisted of 16 rods connected to an electric cord inside a drying hood. In 1929, she patented a scalp protector, which made the procedure more comfortable. Her inventions were readily adopted by all types of salons.

She co-founded the United Beauty School Owners and Teachers Association in 1945 to help raise professional standards for beauticians. At the age of 77, she fulfilled a lifelong dream by earning a bachelor's degree in psychology from Bethune-Cookman College in Florida. Marjorie also received an honorary doctorate in humanities from the college.

She died in 1994 in Illinois at the age of 98.

PERCY LAVON JULIAN

Foam Fire Extinguisher (Aero-Foam)

Dr Percy Lavon Julian was a chemist who invented a foam fire extinguisher called Aero-Foam.

Percy was born in 1899 in Alabama, US. He received little schooling as a child but graduated first in his class at DePauw University in Indiana and went on to earn his master's degree at Harvard University in Massachusetts. After travelling abroad for several years, he received his postgraduate degree from the University of Vienna in Austria in 1931.

His research work at both educational and corporate institutions led to the chemical synthesis (the process of chemical reactions to form a product) of drugs, such as cortisone from soybeans to treat rheumatoid arthritis and other painful conditions. His chemical synthesis process helped to reduce the price of cortisone. Through this work, he invented Aero-Foam, a product that uses soy protein to make a fire-extinguishing foam. It was widely used in World War II (1939-1945) to put out oil and gasoline fires.

Percy created other soybean-based inventions and established his own laboratory, Julian Laboratories, in 1954. He sold the company in 1961, which made him one of the first Black millionaires in the country. He went on to establish the Julian Research Institute, which he ran for the rest of his life.

In 1973, he became the first Black chemist elected to the National Academy of the Sciences, and his chemical synthesis process was recognised by the American Chemical Society as one of the top 25 achievements in the history of American chemistry.

Percy died in 1975 in Illinois at the age of 76.

MARY BEATRICE DAVIDSON KENNER

Sanitary Products

Mary Beatrice Davidson Kenner was a government office worker and entrepreneur who invented sanitary products for women.

She was born in 1912 in North Carolina, US, and along with her sister, Mildred Davidson Austin Smith (see contents page), came from a family of inventors. Their father, Sidney Nathaniel Davidson, invented a portable clothes press in 1914, and their maternal grandfather, Robert Phromeberger, invented a tricolour light signal for trains and a stretcher with wheels for ambulances.

Mary and Mildred did not have technical education, but they were able to spot ways to make peoples' lives better. From a young age, Mary would find solutions to everyday problems. In 1924, her family moved to Washington, DC, and during World War II (1939-1945) she worked for the government.

In 1956, she submitted a patent for a belt to hold sanitary pads in place before stick-on pads were invented in the 1970s. She also invented a moisture-proof pocket to go under the sanitary pad to prevent leakage.

In 1950, Mary left government work and opened her own chain of florists around Washington, DC. She continued to invent things, inspired by her needs around the home. In 1959, she patented an attachment for a walker, composed of a hard-surfaced tray and soft pocket for carrying items, to help her sister be more mobile when she developed multiple sclerosis. In 1982, she patented a toilet paper holder dispenser and went on to invent a mounted back scrubber and washer, a disposable ashtray holder, and a convertible top for car rumble seats (a fold-up seat at the back of a car).

Mary died in 2006 in Washington, DC at the age of 93.

THATO KGATLHANYE

Solar-powered School Bag

Thato Kgatlhanye is an entrepreneur who invented solar-powered school bags.

Born in 1995 in South Africa, Thato was interested in business from a young age, not just for profit but from an ethical standpoint. She graduated from the Vega School of Brand Leadership in South Africa and obtained an internship in New York, US, with Seth Godin, an American marketing guru and author.

In 2013, at the age of 18, Thato co-founded a company called Rethaka, which makes recycled plastic shopping bags into school bags. The bags are solar powered and can be used as a source of light for up to 12 hours. This helps children who do not have electricity at home to be able to study and do homework in the evenings.

The bag is also designed with retroreflective material, which shines light back at a light source. This is helpful in keeping children safe from car accidents as they walk home in the dark on roads with poor, or no, street lighting – a car's light beam shining on the retroreflective material reflects light back and the children can be seen.

Thato's business supplies products to large companies such as Standard Bank, Red Bull, PricewaterhouseCoopers, and Unilever. Her school bags are exported to other countries in Africa and around the world.

LEWIS HOWARD LATIMER

Carbon Filament Light Bulb (improvement)

Lewis Howard Latimer was a draughtsman, patent consultant, and engineer who invented the light bulb with a carbon filament.

He was born in 1848 in Massachusetts, US, and joined the US Navy during the American Civil War (1861-1865) when he was 16 years old, lying about his age as he was too young to join at the time.

When he returned home, Lewis worked at a patent law office where he taught himself mechanical drawing. During his career as a draughtsman and patent consultant, he worked closely with famous inventors, assisting them in the development of some of the world's most important inventions. He helped Alexander Graham Bell draft the patent for his design of the telephone. He also worked with Thomas Edison and Hiram Maxim, who were competitors in the field of lighting, where he used his skills in patenting and electrical engineering to explain their inventions.

He invented an improvement to Thomas Edison's original paper filament light bulb, which burned out too quickly. Lewis's lightbulb, which used a carbon filament instead, was patented in 1881. It was longer-lasting and made electric lighting more affordable. He sold his patent to the US Electric Lighting Company, which was founded by Hiram Maxim, and worked there to supervise the installation of public electric lights on streets and roads in the US, Canada, and the UK.

In 1884, Thomas Edison invited Lewis to work for him, and he joined the Edison Electric Light Company as a patent investigator and expert witness.

Lewis published his book *Incandescent Electric Lighting: A Practical Description of the Edison System* in 1890. He also designed an improved railway carriage bathroom. In addition to his draughting skills, he enjoyed other creative pastimes, including playing the flute and writing poetry and plays.

He died in 1928 in New York at the age of 80.

GERALD (JERRY) LAWSON

Home Video Game Console

Gerald Lawson was an engineer and game designer who pioneered the first home video game console with game cartridges.

Known as Jerry, he was born in 1940 in New York, US. He was interested in electronics from a young age and was a self-taught engineer. He was also enterprising from a young age and made money by fixing neighbours' electronics and repairing their televisions.

Jerry's interest in computing led him to Silicon Valley in California, where many major innovative technology, software and Internet companies are based. He worked on military devices, focusing mainly on aircraft displays, and was one of the few Black engineers working in computing at the time.

In the 1970s, he worked on designing the Fairchild Channel F Console, which was the first cartridge-based home video game console system. His work paved the way for later home video game console systems, such as the Atari 2600, Nintendo, Xbox, and PlayStation.

Jerry died in 2011 in California at the age of 70.

ELIJAH McCOY

Engine Automatic Lubricator

Elijah McCoy was a mechanical engineer who invented an automatic lubricating device to keep engines continuously oiled.

Elijah was born in 1844 in Ontario, Canada. His parents were from Kentucky, US, and the family later returned to the US and settled in Michigan. He showed a strong interest in mechanics from a young age, and his parents arranged for him to travel to Scotland at the age of 15 for an apprenticeship in mechanical engineering.

When he returned, he worked for the Michigan Central Railroad as a fireman and oiler. His duties included lubricating engine parts with oil, which led him to develop his first major inventions. Engines needed frequent lubrication and, each time, the trains had to be stopped and started for this work to be done. Elijah invented a lubricating cup that distributed oil evenly over the engine's moving parts, allowing trains to run continuously for long periods without having to stop for maintenance.

He continued to improve his devices and received nearly 60 patents, most of which related to lubrication systems. Soon, long-distance trains, ships, and factory machines were using his lubricating invention. His reputation spread, and he led a very successful career as a sought-after engineer.

In 1920, he founded the Elijah McCoy Manufacturing Company to produce lubricators branded with his name. Heavy equipment users often asked for 'the real McCoy', a phrase that still exists in today's vocabulary, to make sure that they were not buying cheaper and less effective lubricators.

Elijah died in 1929 in Michigan at the age of 85.

ANNIE MINERVA TURNBO MALONE

Hair Care Products

Annie Minerva Turnbo Malone was an entrepreneur and pioneer in the beauty and cosmetic business who created hair care products to help Black women straighten their hair.

Born in 1869 in Illinois, US, Annie was fascinated by hair and chemistry, and with the guidance of her aunt (a herbalist who used plants for healing) she began experimenting with hair products.

One of her first inventions was a liquid shampoo (in the olden days, people would use lye soap made of strong chemicals or water to wash their hair). She was also interested in finding a way to straighten hair without damaging the hair follicles. She experimented with gentler chemicals and created a hair straightening formula, which she called her Wonderful Hair Grower.

Annie was one of the most successful entrepreneurs in America at the time. She was the first known Black woman to become a self-made millionaire by launching a hair care business empire. She also helped to provide meaningful career opportunities for other Black women. At one point, she employed Madam CJ Walker (see contents page) as a hair care sales agent, who also became well-known and successful in the same line of business.

She helped to popularise beauty and cosmetology schools. By the 1950s, 32 branches of her Poro Cosmetology School were up and running across the country. Her Poro system taught women about the importance of scalp health as well as hair styling. She recommended regularly washing hair using a sulphur-based treatment, improving diet, and practising head massage to heal hair follicle problems.

Annie died in 1957 in Illinois at the age of 88.

NEWMAN RUSSELL MARSHMAN

Typewriter (improvement)

Newman Russell Marshman was a music professor who co-invented the improved typewriter.

Newman was born in 1846 in New York, US. He worked as a professor of music and invented musical instruments, including an organette – a small, portable reed organ that played mechanically by turning a crank handle. It was one of the first affordable instruments for recorded music. Using the same principle, he also invented a flute organ and player harmonica, whereby music was created by a series of holes punched into a roll of paper. By blowing into the mouthpiece, sound and music were created while turning handles to wind the paper roll through the instrument.

Newman moved on to invent toys and is especially known for creating the toy theatre or 'Punch and Judy Show', a traditional puppet show that was very popular at the time.

In 1882, he created inventions in partnership with another inventor, Lee Burridge. Together, they devised the Sun Index Typewriter, which worked without a keyboard. They went on to perfect a type-bar typewriter by simplifying the parts and movements, and it was cheaper to produce than the original typewriter.

Newman became a successful typewriter manufacturer as well as a typewriter designer. He later also devised adding machines and a cash register.

He died in 1930 in New York at the age of 83.

THOMAS MARTIN

Fire Extinguisher/Engine

Thomas Martin invented the fire extinguisher or engine.

Thomas was living in Michigan, US, in 1872, when his invention was patented.

His fire extinguisher invention was a pipe and valves design, and not the wall-hanging type. It used a stationary engine or motor to pump water from a reservoir to prevent or put out a fire. The nature of his invention related to the construction, arrangement, and combination of pipes and valves for conducting water from suitable reservoirs to burning buildings and other structures.

Thomas's fire extinguisher was also used to warn of fires through the sounding of an alarm, ventilate to dissipate smoke, and wash buildings, pavements, and roads.

WASHINGTON MARTIN

Lock (improvement)

Washington Martin was an inventor who designed an improved lock.

He was born in 1948 and was living in Illinois, US, when he applied for the patent for his invention.

His lock was an improvement on the bolt lock originally invented by the Chinese more than 4,000 years ago. It was a mechanical device which could be used with keys or number locks and consisted of a cylinder and spiral spring coiled around a metal pin.

Washington's invention was patented in 1889, and its design is the basis of modern door locks used today.

JAN ERNST MATZELIGER

Shoe-lasting Machine

Jan Ernst Matzeliger worked in a shoe factory and invented the shoe-lasting machine, which is a machine that makes shoes.

Born in 1852 in Dutch Guiana, now called Suriname, in South America, he showed interest in mechanics from a young age. Jan travelled the world as a sailor on an East Indian merchant ship and settled in Massachusetts, US, after finding a position as an apprentice in a shoe factory.

He learned the cordwaining trade, which is the crafting of shoes almost entirely by hand. It is considered the most difficult and time-consuming stage of shoe assembly, and Jan decided to find an easier way to do this work. After experimenting with different designs, he invented the shoe-lasting machine.

His machine held a shoe on a last (a tool shaped like a foot), pulled the leather down around the heel, set and drove in the nails, and released the completed shoe. It was able to produce 700 pairs of shoes a day, more than ten times the amount normally produced by hand at the time.

In 1889, Jan was one of the founders of the Consolidated Lasting Machine Company, which began to manufacture his invention. The shoe-lasting machine increased shoe production tremendously and was an immediate success. It led to the employment of more unskilled workers who could easily operate the machine, and an increase in low-cost, high-quality footwear for people all around the world.

He died in 1889 in Massachusetts at the age of 36.

THOMAS MENSAH

Fibre Optics Technologies

Dr Thomas Mensah is a chemical engineer and entrepreneur who pioneered fibre optics manufacturing and communications systems.

Thomas was born in 1950 in Ghana. He excelled in science and maths and could speak French fluently. He received a bachelor's degree in chemical engineering from the Kwame Nkrumah University of Science and Technology in Ghana in 1974. He continued his studies at Montpellier University in France, where he received a postgraduate degree in chemical engineering in 1978.

In 1980, Thomas started working as a research engineer in the US. He showed a remarkable ability in understanding chemical qualities for improving manufacturing processes. By 1983, he had made improvements to the process of making fibre optic cables, which contain strands of glass fibres, provide higher bandwidth, and transmit data over longer distances than wired cables.

He also led in the design of advanced laser-guided weapons, installing a small camera in the missiles' noses, which helped pilots to lock onto targets with incredible accuracy. He developed aerospace innovations and founded Supercond Technologies, a high-tech company specialising in developing advanced structural materials for supersonic fighter aircraft.

Thomas holds seven patents for fibre optics technologies, three in fibre optic guided missile technology and four in manufacturing fibre optics inexpensively, which has greatly revolutionised telecommunications (the exchange of information over a distance, such as by telephone) and the Internet.

He has received many awards for his technological achievements throughout his career.

ALEXANDER MILES

Automatic Elevator Doors

Alexander Miles was a businessman who invented elevator doors that open and close automatically.

Born in 1938 in Minnesota, US, he moved to Wisconsin, where he worked as a barber and experimented with making hair products. He returned to Minnesota, where he managed a barber shop in a hotel.

Alexander also started a real estate business and developed an area in Duluth, Minnesota, which became known as the Miles Block, a development of business and retail buildings named after him. He later became the first Black member of the Duluth Chamber of Commerce in Minnesota.

He was inspired to work on elevator door mechanisms while riding an elevator with his young daughter and seeing the risk involved with elevator shaft doors that did not close properly.

This led Alexander to design elevator doors that opened and closed automatically – before that, riding an elevator was complicated and could be dangerous, as people had to shut both the shaft doors and elevator doors manually before riding the elevator, or risk falling down the elevator shaft. He patented his automatic elevator doors in 1889, and his design is still used in modern elevators today.

In 1899, he and his family moved to Illinois, where he founded the United Brotherhood, a life insurance company for Black people who could not get coverage from other insurance companies. Through the successes of his ventures, he became known as the wealthiest Black man in the 'Northwest'.

Alexander died in 1918 in Washington at the age of 79.

BENJAMIN THORNTON MONTGOMERY

Shallow Water Steamboat Propeller

Benjamin Thornton Montgomery was a businessman and inventor who designed the shallow water steamboat propeller.

He was born in 1819 in Virginia, US, and later moved to Mississippi. His employer recognised his intelligence at a young age, and he was given the responsibility of running the general store on the plantation on which he grew up. He was a skilled mechanic and learnt techniques for land surveying, flood control, and the draughting of architectural plans.

Benjamin also oversaw purchasing and shipping operations on the plantation. During that time, merchandise was normally transported by boats along rivers connecting counties and states. With the differences in water depths along the rivers, navigation could be difficult, and this could delay deliveries if boats got stuck. He decided to fix this problem by designing a special propeller for boats that cut into the water at different angles. This allowed a boat to navigate more easily through shallow waters.

After the American Civil War (1861-1865), he bought the plantation on which he lived as well as other land and property. He became one of the wealthiest cotton planters in Mississippi and founded a market centre, called Montgomery and Sons, which included a store, several warehouses, and a steam-driven cotton gin and press to process cotton.

Benjamin died in 1877 in Mississippi at the age of 57.

GARRETT AUGUSTUS MORGAN

Smoke Hood/Gas Mask

Garrett Augustus Morgan was a business owner and inventor who created a smoke hood or gas mask to help protect firefighters in burning buildings.

He was born in 1877 in Kentucky, US, received only primary schooling, and moved to Ohio at the age of 14 in search of work. Garrett worked as a handyman for a landowner and then as a sewing machine repairman for a clothing manufacturer. His first invention was an improved sewing machine. He later opened his own sewing machine shop, a shoe repair shop, and a clothing store.

In 1913, he launched the GA Morgan Hair Refining Company, which sold hair products he had invented, including his patented hair straightening cream, hair colouring oil, and a hair straightening comb.

Garrett invented the smoke hood in 1916. This was later modified to carry its own air supply – effectively the first gas mask – which saved many soldiers in both World War I (1914-1918) and World War II (1939-1945), protecting them from poisonous gas used in chemical weapons.

Due to the success of his inventions, he became the first Black person in Ohio to own a car. He witnessed many car accidents at busy road junctions, and this inspired him to improve the two-light traffic system, which only indicated 'stop' (red light) and 'go' (green light). He added a 'yield' component (amber light) to warn drivers of an impending stop. Garrett's three-light traffic light was patented in 1923 and helped to reduce road accidents.

He died in 1963 in Ohio at the age of 86.

LYDA NEWMAN

Hairbrush (improvement)

Lyda Newman was a hairdresser who invented an improved hairbrush design.

She was born in 1885 in Ohio, US.

Lyda worked in Manhattan, New York as a private hairdresser for a family. It was during this time that she developed her concept for a new design of the hairbrush, which included several features for efficiency, hygiene, and ventilation. The hairbrush had evenly spaced rows of bristles with open slots to guide debris away from the hair into a compartment with a back that could be opened at the touch of a button for cleaning.

Some early hairbrushes used hard bristles made from animal hair or porcupine quills, which were harsh on the scalp and hair. Lyda's hairbrush used synthetic bristles, which lasted longer, were cheaper than natural bristles, and were less painful on the scalp. Her improved hairbrush was patented in 1898.

Lyda was also an activist and was one of the organisers of a Black members' branch of the Woman Suffrage Party, which fought for women to have the legal right to vote.

DOLLY NICHOLAS

Emulsion Treatment Process

Dolly Nicholas is a chemist who invented the emulsion treatment process, which treats and breaks down emulsions (a mixture of two or more liquids that do not dissolve together).

Born in 1952 in Trinidad and Tobago in the Caribbean, Dolly earned a bachelor's degree in environmental polymer chemistry at Lakehead University in Canada and a master's degree in analytical chemistry at Queen's University in Canada.

She has worked for various corporations in Trinidad and Tobago and the US, where a key part of her work involved addressing environmental issues associated with asphalt, tar sand, and heavy oil industries.

Dolly invented processes to treat emulsions and waste from the petroleum and petrochemical industry. Her emulsion treatment process separates a tight emulsion into saleable crude oil, which is the base for many products, such as transportation fuels, oils used for heating, and electricity generation.

She holds patents for different commercially useful processes and is passionate about entrepreneurship and innovation. She has also invented a range of coatings, paints, and adhesives marketed under the Lasco brand, a well-known product name in the Caribbean. Her inventions include processes to convert recycled plastics, such as soft drink plastic bottles, into usable products, such as epoxy coatings.

Dolly has received many awards and is the first and only woman to receive a national award for scientific invention in Trinidad and Tobago. She is a member of the Third World Organisation for Women in Science and Scientists without Borders.

AMINA ODIDI and ISA ODIDI

Medicine Delivery System

Dr Isa Odidi and Dr Amina Odidi are husband and wife scientists who created an innovative medicine delivery system.

Amina and Isa were both born in Nigeria. They both hold bachelor's degrees in pharmacy from Ahmadu Bello University in Nigeria, master's degrees in biopharmaceutics, and postgraduate degrees in pharmaceutics from the University of London in the UK.

Isa also holds an MBA (Masters in Business Administration) from the University of Toronto in Canada. He has held senior positions in academia, and his work has been cited in textbooks. He has published over a hundred scientific and medical papers, articles, and textbooks.

Amina has developed and applied technologies to the development of controlled-release medical prescription products, which allow patients to take a prescription once a day instead of many times a day. This makes it easier for patients to manage and follow doctors' orders on medication.

They both work in the pharmaceutical and healthcare industries and have co-invented various delivery devices for foods that provide medical or health benefits. In 1998, Amina and Isa co-founded Intellipharmaceutics, a successful pharmaceutical company specialising in the research, development, and manufacture of controlled-release and targeted-release oral solid dosage medical prescriptions (medicines in the form of tablets or capsules).

In 2004, their company received the Harry Jerome Award for Technology and Innovation presented by the Black Business and Professional Association in Canada.

GODFREY (GEOFF) HENRY OLIVER PALMER

Barley Abrasion Process

Sir Godfrey Henry Oliver Palmer is a university professor and grain scientist who invented the barley abrasion process.

Known as Geoff, he was born in 1940 in Jamaica in the Caribbean and moved to England when he was 14 years old. He earned a bachelor's degree in botany at the University of Leicester in 1964, a master's degree at the University of Nottingham, and a postgraduate degree in grain science and technology jointly at Heriot-Watt University and the University of Edinburgh in Scotland in 1967. He received a doctorate in science from Heriot-Watt University in 1985.

Geoff patented the barley abrasion process in 1969, which converts barley into malt through mechanical abrasion to give a more efficient malting process. This was used by the British beer brewing industry, giving the UK a huge competitive advantage in beer brewing for many decades.

Under his direction, Heriot-Watt University established its unique International Centre for Brewing and Distilling, which continues to attract students from around the world. He is also one of the founders of the Scottish Brewing Archive at the University of Glasgow, which holds historical information on Scottish brewing.

In 1998, Geoff became the fourth person – and the first person from Europe – to be honoured with the American Society of Brewing Chemists Award of Distinction, which is considered the Nobel Prize of brewing. In 2002, he received the Good Citizenship Award of Edinburgh for exceptional contributions to community work and good race relations. In 2003, he received an OBE (Officer of the Most Excellent Order of the British Empire), awarded by the Queen, for his contribution to grain science.

On his retirement in 2005, he was made Emeritus Professor of Heriot-Watt University. Geoff was knighted in 2014 for his services to human rights, science, and charity.

ALICE PARKER

Heating System

Alice Parker was a cook who invented a heating system using natural gas.

She was born in 1895 in Virginia, US and attended classes at Howard University Academy, a high school affiliated with Howard University in Washington, DC. Alice worked as a private cook at a home in New Jersey.

She designed her heating system because she felt that her fireplace was not effective enough to warm her whole house during cold winters. Her invention allowed cool air to be drawn into a heater or boiler, conveyed through a heat exchanger, and the warmed air to be delivered through ducts or vents to individual rooms in a house. This was an early form of central heating.

Alice's unique design used natural gas as its fuel instead of coal or wood, which was convenient because it meant that people did not have to go outside to chop wood or buy coal. It also reduced the risk of house fires from leaving a burning fireplace on throughout the night, which is what people did to keep their house warm.

Her design was patented in 1919 and is recognised as a revolutionary invention that saved energy and led the way for modern central heating systems used in houses and other buildings today.

Alice died in 1920 in New Jersey at the age of 25.

JAMES ALBERT PARSONS

Rust-resistant Metals

James Albert Parsons was a metallurgist (a person who studies or knows about metals) and scientist who patented his work on rust-resistant metals.

Born in 1900 in Ohio, US, James graduated from Rensselaer Polytechnic Institute in New York in 1922, where he studied electrical engineering. He spent most of his working life at Duriron Company in Ohio, which manufactured metals.

James developed rust-resistant and non-corrosive metals, and this led to the development of stainless steel, which does not rust and is hard-wearing. Between 1929 and 1949, he received eight patents relating to the development and application of non-corrosive metals, which were credited to Duriron. In 1935, Duriron was known as the world's only manufacturer of specific kinds of non-corrosive metals.

He was regarded as one of the country's leading metallurgists. In 1951, he left Duriron and joined the faculty at Tennessee State University where he taught until 1967.

James died in 1989 in Ohio at the age of 88.

CHARLES (RICH) RICHARD PATTERSON
(and son FREDERICK DOUGLAS PATTERSON)

Vehicle Manufacturing

Charles Richard Patterson owned an automobile manufacturing company, which rivalled the Ford Motor Company at the time. He and his son, Frederick Douglas Patterson, designed and built their own vehicles.

Charles – who was known as Rich – was born in 1833 in Virginia, US. He was a blacksmith by trade – someone who shapes and joins metals to make useful items, such as tools and furniture.

Just before the American Civil War (1861-1865), Rich headed north and began working at a carriage company in Ohio, where he used his blacksmithing skills to make some of the finest and most popular horse-driven carriages in the late 1800s. He eventually took over the business and formed the CR Patterson and Sons Carriage Company, which became the country's only Black-owned automobile manufacturing company.

After Rich's death in Ohio in 1910 at the age of 73, his son, Frederick (1871-1932), took over the business and started building motor vehicles in competition with the Ford Motor Company, owned by Henry Ford. Frederick had been trained in the family business from a young age and was a natural mechanic who built some of his own designs. He was the first Black person to graduate from a local high school and the first Black man on Ohio State University's football team.

His first cars – the Patterson-Greenfield touring car and a roadster version – were considered mechanically superior to Henry Ford's first car, the Ford Model T.

Frederick's business moved on to become the Greenfield Bus Body Company, which produced the first trucks, buses, and two-wheeled trailers in the 1920s and 30s.

WILLIAM PURVIS

Fountain Pen

William Purvis was a business owner who designed the fountain pen.

He was born in 1838 in Pennsylvania, US, received little education, and was mostly self-taught. His earliest patent, in 1883, was an improvement to a hand stamp, which self-inked through an attached ink reservoir. He also patented a bag fastener and invented the edge cutter found on aluminium foil, cling film wrap, and wax paper boxes today.

William had a particular interest in paper bags and continually worked on improving the bag-making process. From 1884 to 1897, he was granted at least six different patents for paper bag technology, and in 1885, he founded the Sterling Paper Bag Company to manufacture his bags.

In 1890, he received a patent for his fountain pen. William found it inconvenient to have to carry around a bottle of ink whenever he needed to use a pen, which led him to invent the fountain pen. He designed a mechanism involving an elastic tube to connect the ink reservoir and pen tip. Suction and pressure within the elastic tube regulated the flow of ink while writing with the pen, which prevented ink leaks or faded writing from either too much or too little ink flowing through.

William also patented three designs for the electric train, including a closed conduit electric railway system which set an electromagnet under the centre of the railway carriage to balance it. In 1901, he formed the Union Electric Construction Company in New York to manufacture these inventions.

He died in 1914 in Pennsylvania at the age of 75.

MARK RICHARDS

Air Quality Monitor

Dr Mark Richards is an atmospheric physicist and university lecturer who developed the air quality monitor.

He was born in 1970 in England to parents who were from Jamaica in the Caribbean. He holds a bachelor's degree in chemistry from the University of Manchester and a postgraduate degree in atmospheric physics from Imperial College London.

When he was young, Mark could not find many Black scientists as role models. He discovered a book called *Blacks in Science* by Ivan Van Sertima and was particularly inspired by Imhotep, an Egyptian polymath (a person with a wide knowledge of a large number of subjects) who excelled in so many areas – including engineering, architecture, medicine, astronomy, and music – thousands of years ago.

As an atmospheric physicist, Mark uses physics to study and understand the Earth's atmosphere. He researched air pollution in urban areas, which are heavily populated and have heavy traffic, and this led to his invention of the air quality monitor. He co-founded Duvas Technologies, a high-tech business that develops air pollution monitoring instruments to monitor and map air quality in real-time (similar to a weather map but for air pollution).

Mark has shared his experiences with many young people through initiatives in the UK, the US, the Caribbean, and Africa to inspire and encourage them to study science, technology, engineering, and maths (STEM) and pursue careers as scientists.

NORBERT RILLIEUX

Sugar-Refining Machine

Norbert Rillieux was an engineer who invented a sugar-refining machine to produce better quality sugar from sugar cane.

Born in 1806 in Louisiana, US, he received a good education and was sent to study at L'Ecole Centrale in France, a research institution for engineering and science. He became an instructor there in 1830 in applied mechanics and published papers on steam engines and steam power.

Norbert also began working on an evaporator to try to find a more efficient way of refining sugar cane juice. Before that, workers had to spoon boiling sugar juice from one open pot to another, which was dangerous and produced a lower quality sugar as the heat in the pots could not be regulated, and a lot of the sugar was lost in the process of transferring the juice.

He returned to Louisiana in the early 1830s, where he further developed his sugar-refining machine. His multiple-effect evaporator double-refined sugar to produce better-quality sugar crystals through the evaporation of moisture from sugar cane juice while controlling the heat applied. It was patented in 1943. His invention increased sugar production, reduced production costs, and protected lives by ending the older, dangerous methods. The evaporators were very efficient and profitable for sugar-makers.

In the 1850s, there was an outbreak of yellow fever in New Orleans, Louisiana, caused by mosquitos carrying the disease. Norbert devised an elaborate plan for eliminating the outbreak by draining the swamplands surrounding the city and improving the existing sewer system, thereby removing the breeding ground for the insects.

He returned to France in the late 1850s and became interested in Egyptology and hieroglyphics. In 1881, he adapted his multiple-effect evaporation system to extract sugar from sugar beets.

Norbert died in 1894 in France at the age of 88.

LEVI ROOTS (KEITH GRAHAM)

Reggae Reggae Sauce

Levi Roots is an entrepreneur, musician, and celebrity chef who created the Reggae Reggae Sauce, a jerk chicken sauce inspired by his Jamaican heritage.

He was born Keith Graham in 1958 in Jamaica in the Caribbean, where he grew up helping out on the family farm. He later changed his name to Levi Roots to better reflect his background and culture.

When he was still young, his parents moved to England. They could not afford to take all of their children with them so each year they would send for one of them. As the youngest, Levi was the last to be sent for, so he got to spend the most time with his beloved grandmother. They sang and cooked in the kitchen, where she taught him the secrets of Caribbean cooking.

Levi moved to London at the age of 11. He missed the music and sunshine in Jamaica, and as he grew up this inspired him to create a special hot sauce to remind him of the Caribbean. He decided to sell his sauce and peddled each batch around Brixton on his bike. He also sold it at food markets and exhibitions, and at a food stall at the Notting Hill Carnival.

He was spotted at an exhibition by one of the producers of the BBC reality television show *Dragons' Den*, and was invited to present his sauce on the show to try to get funding to expand his business. He became one of their biggest success stories and was able to launch his sauce nationally.

Levi perfected and refined his hot sauce to create his Reggae Reggae Sauce. After the show, supermarket chain Sainsbury's agreed to an exclusive distribution deal. Within weeks, his sauce was on store shelves and in huge demand. Now, it is stocked by all the major retailers, and he has built a complete brand of food and drink products, ranging from ready meals to snacks, soft drinks, and Caribbean pasties.

His success has made him a spokesperson for Caribbean cuisine as well as for entrepreneurship in the Black community. He has visited hundreds of schools to encourage young children to adopt a positive attitude to life, while proving that a person can succeed from humble beginnings.

ARCHIA ROSS

Doorstep/Stair Runner

Archia Ross was a store owner who invented a runner to be used on doorsteps and stairs.

Archia was living in New York, US when he received the patent for his invention in 1896. He owned a store in Manhattan, selling wardrobe fixtures for hanging clothes.

His doorstep runner invention helped to prevent slips and falls on icy or wet pavements. It could be used in both private and public places and on stairs. The basic design was a series of interlocking mats. The runner could be removed when not needed and easily stored away until needed again.

Archia's other inventions included a bag closure device in 1898, which allowed for the removal of waste rubbish from a home or business without spillage. The mouth of the bag hung open for easy filling, and once filled, the bag closure sealed the opening.

In 1899, he received a patent for his trouser support or stretcher. It had several hooks that allowed for trousers to be hung without being folded, which stopped them from getting wrinkled. In 1903, he invented a clothes hanger for trousers and skirts that consisted of eyelets, loops, and arms used to fasten the clothing. He also designed a holder for brooms that attached to a wall and could hold a number of items.

Archia died in 1910 in New Hampshire.

JESSE EUGENE RUSSELL

Digital Mobile Phone Technology

Jesse Eugene Russell is an electrical engineer and IT entrepreneur who pioneered digital mobile phone technology.

He was born in 1948 in Tennessee, US, and received his bachelor's degree in electrical engineering from Tennessee State University, and his master's degree in electrical engineering from Stanford University in California.

Jesse was the first Black person to be hired by Bell Laboratories – a large research company that develops a wide range of technologies – directly from a historically Black university. Historically Black Colleges and Universities (HBCU) were originally established to serve the educational needs of Black people who had been previously excluded from a post-secondary education.

Jesse holds over 100 patents. In the 1980s, he led the team that pioneered digital mobile phone technology, called the 2G or 'second generation' of mobile phone systems. Before that, mobile phones used an analogue system which has more distortion, noise, and interference than a digital system.

In the 1990s, he received patents for base station technology, which transmits radio wave signals to and from mobile devices.

Jesse has received a number of awards and was named US Black Engineer of the Year in 1992.

WILLIAM SACHITI

Kar-go (Driverless Car)

William Sachiti is an entrepreneur who developed an electric car called Kar-go, that can drive without a driver, to deliver multiple packages to different destinations.

Born Pasihapaori Chidziva in 1985 in Zimbabwe, William moved to the UK when he was 16 years old, and started out as an entrepreneur at the age of 19 with a website domain name registration business called '123-registration'.

He appeared on the BBC reality television show *Dragons' Den* to try to get funding for his company, Clever Bins, a digital advertising platform using solar power on high-tech street bins, designed to attract attention in busy cities. While he did not receive the funding, his company successfully licensed its technology to six countries and local governments. In 2013, he founded MyCityVenue, a digital concierge and holiday company which had around 1.6 million users.

William went on to study artificial intelligence and robotics at the University of Aberystwyth in Wales, where he invented the world's first robot librarian, named Hugh. Hugh could hold a conversation, follow instructions, and direct people to any one of several million books in the library.

While at the university, William worked with a team of scientists to find a way to deliver packages independently. He founded the Academy of Robotics, a vehicle manufacturing company, and developed Kar-go, a driverless car for last-mile delivery (the final delivery destination) by using advanced robotics and driverless vehicle technology.

Kar-go works in conjunction with an app on which people can track their deliveries and meet the vehicle. They then use the app to open the vehicle door to release their parcels through a patented package management system that sorts and re-shuffles packages. Kar-go is powered by Tesla batteries, can drive at 96 kilometres (60 miles) per hour, and cover around 193 kilometres (120 miles) before it needs recharging.

William has won awards for his various inventions. In 2017, he was named one of the top '35 under 35' entrepreneurs in Wales.

OMOWUNMI SADIK

Bomb Detector Biosensor

Dr Omowunmi Sadik is a surface chemist and lecturer who invented biosensors that detect bombs, explosives, or drugs.

Omowunmi was born in 1964 in Nigeria. She was interested in the sciences at school and earned her bachelor's and master's degrees in chemistry at the University of Lagos in Nigeria, and her postgraduate degree in chemistry at Wollongong University in Australia. She has held teaching appointments in the US at Harvard University in Massachusetts, at Cornell University and Binghamton University in New York, and at the Naval Research Laboratory in Washington, DC.

As a surface chemist. Omowunmi deals with the properties of surfaces and the chemical changes that occur on a surface. Her research areas are in chemical sensors and biosensors, and their application to solving real-life problems in biological systems, energy, and the environment. She holds patents for microelectrode biosensors that detect foreign materials, and can be used to detect bombs, explosives, or hard drugs.

In 2012, she co-founded the Sustainable Nanotechnology Organisation, an international professional society for the responsible use of nanotechnology worldwide. Nanotechnology is the science of working with something on the microscopic level to create something useful.

Omowunmi was awarded the Nigerian National Order of Merit for Science in 2016 and has received fellowships at the American Institute for Medical and Biological Engineering, the Royal Society of Chemistry, and the National Research Council.

SAMUEL RAYMOND SCOTTRON

Dual Adjusting Mirror

Samuel Raymond Scottron was a barber and entrepreneur who designed the dual adjusting mirror.

He was born in 1841 in Pennsylvania, US, and moved with his family to New York when he was young. Samuel worked as a barber with his father, and also in the family business, selling goods to soldiers during the American Civil War (1861-1865). He moved to Florida in 1864, where he started a chain of grocery stores. Soon after, he sold his grocery stores and moved to Massachusetts, where he opened a barber shop.

He created the dual adjustable mirror on a standing pole to help his customers to see the back of their head after having their hair cut and styled in his barber shop. His invention was called the Scottron Mirror and was patented in 1868.

Samuel moved back to New York, studied at the Cooper Union College, and graduated with a degree in algebra and engineering in 1875.

He created many other inventions, including an adjustable window cornice board to hide curtain rods in 1880, a curtain pole tip in 1886, a curtain rod in 1892, a supporting bracket for curtains in 1893, and a leather hand strap device used for support when standing in trams and other forms of public transportation. In 1894, he perfected a way to make glass look like onyx (a black semi-precious gemstone) for using in decorative and ornamental items.

His inventions would eventually make him a wealthy man. He became involved in race-related issues and local politics and wrote about this for various newspapers and magazines.

Samuel died in 1908 in New York at the age of 67.

MARY JANE GRANT SEACOLE

Herbal Remedies

Mary Jane Grant Seacole was a pioneering nurse and businesswoman who created herbal remedies.

She was born in 1805 in Jamaica in the Caribbean. From a young age, she was interested in medicine and nursing. Her mother was a healer skilled in traditional medicine who kept a boarding house for injured soldiers. From the age of 12, Mary helped her mother in her work.

She loved travelling and visiting other parts of the Caribbean, Central America, and England, where she learnt how people used local plants and herbs to treat the sick. She used a combination of traditional Jamaican treatments and remedies and European medical ideas to heal people, and was widely praised for her work during a cholera epidemic in Panama, and for her treatment of tropical diseases, such as yellow fever.

In 1854, Mary travelled to England to offer her services as an army nurse in the Crimean War (1853-1856) in Europe, but she was turned down. Undeterred, she travelled to Crimea with a relative, and they set up the British Hotel to sell food, supplies, and medicine to the troops. She helped wounded soldiers in military hospitals and on the battlefields, where she became well-known as 'Mother Seacole'. She created natural herbal remedies when other medicines were not easily available, grinding plants and herbs with a pestle and mortar, mixing them in a bowl or putting them in a pan over a fire. Remedies like these are still used today.

After the Crimean War, Mary returned to England. She received many medals from governments of different countries for her bravery and work during the war. In 1857, her autobiography, *Wonderful Adventures of Mrs Seacole in Many Lands*, was published and became a bestseller. In 1871, Prince Victor of Hohenlohe-Lagenburg, a sculptor who was a nephew of Queen Victoria, made a statue of her which was exhibited at the Royal Academy summer exhibition in 1872.

She died in 1881 in London at the age of 75.

PETER SESAY

Seat Belt Height Adjuster

Peter Sesay was a car safety expert who invented the Autosafe Seat Belt Height Adjuster, a seat belt for children.

He lived in the UK and patented his invention in 1999.

Peter presented his idea on the BBC reality television show *Dragons'*
Den and was successful in getting funding and support for his invention,
which allowed seat belts to be easily adjusted to suit a child's height.
Normal car seat belts are made to fit adults, and they usually rub against
a child's neck, so they end up being moved away or tucked under the
child's arm instead, which leaves their upper body unprotected and
vulnerable to injury.

His invention had a special buckle for guiding two belts. It had a space
for the first belt to run through, a second space for the second belt to
run through, and the two spaces joined at a meeting point. The second
belt could be easily inserted or removed from the second space for
adjustment by tightening or loosening. This device kept the seat belt
away from children's necks to stop it from harming them.

Peter's invention sold well in various retail outlets. It increased the safety
of seat belts by fitting them properly to children's bodies, which reduced
injuries and made car journeys safer.

MILDRED DAVIDSON AUSTIN SMITH

Board Game (Family Treedition)

Mildred Davidson Austin Smith was an inventor who designed a board game called *Family Treedition*.

Born 1916 in North Carolina, US, she and her sister, Mary Beatrice Davidson Kenner (see contents page), came from a family of inventors. Their father, Sidney Nathaniel Davidson, invented a portable clothes press in 1914, and their maternal grandfather, Robert Phromeberger, invented a tricolour light signal for trains and a stretcher with wheels for ambulances.

Mildred and Mary did not have a technical education, but they were both exceptional at spotting ways to make peoples' lives better.

At a young age, Mildred became ill with multiple sclerosis (a condition that can affect the brain and spinal cord, causing a wide range of symptoms). While she was bedridden, she created a children's board game that explored family ties, which she called *Family Treedition*. She trademarked this name in 1980.

The game was mainly designed for young people to help them understand their place in their extended families, but it also became popular with adults. The board game was manufactured in several versions, including Braille (a system of touch reading for blind people in which raised dots on paper represent the letters of the alphabet).

Mildred was also known as a professional opera singer in North Carolina.

She died in 1993 at the age of 76.

VALERIE THOMAS

Illusion Transmitter

Dr Valerie Thomas is a scientist who created the illusion transmitter, which produces realistic, three-dimensional (3D) images.

She was born in 1943 in Maryland, US and showed an aptitude and fascination for science and technology at a young age. She excelled in her studies and was one of only two women to major in physics at Morgan State University in Maryland at the time.

In 1964, Valerie began a lifelong career at NASA (National Aeronautics and Space Administration) as a data analyst. In the 1970s, she managed the development of image-processing systems for Landsat, the first satellite to send images to Earth from space. She helped to develop computer programme designs that supported research on Halley's Comet (the famous comet that comes close to Earth around every 75 years), the ozone layer, and satellite technology. Throughout her career, she contributed widely to the study of space.

In 1980, Valerie received a patent for her illusion transmitter, which uses concave mirrors and rays of light to produce optical illusion images. It has contributed greatly to research at NASA and has since been adapted for use in other 3D technologies, including modern medical imaging, 3D film, and 3D television.

She has received a number of awards from NASA. Her success as a scientist also inspired her to reach out to students and she has mentored young people through various initiatives.

DOX THRASH

Carborundum Printmaking Process

Dox Thrash was an artist, draughtsman, and printmaker who co-invented the carborundum printmaking process.

He was born in 1893 in Georgia, US. From a very young age, Dox wanted to be an artist, and he enrolled in art correspondence courses. When he was 15 years old, he started performing with travelling circuses and variety shows. He moved to Illinois at the age of 17 and did odd jobs as an elevator operator and railway porter.

In 1914, he enrolled at the Art Institute of Chicago and received private tutoring from William Scott, a British artist who visited the US. In 1917, during World War I (1914-1918), Dox joined the US Army where he served in France in an all-Black unit. After the war, he resumed his studies at the Art Institute of Chicago.

He moved to New York during the Harlem Renaissance, an intellectual, social, and artistic movement in the 1920s. During this time, he painted the people of America, especially Black people. In 1926, he settled in Philadelphia. He made his debut as an artist in 1931 with an exhibition of his paintings, and held his first print exhibition in 1933.

In 1937, during the American Depression, Dox joined the Federal Arts Project as a printmaker and discovered that carborundum mezzotint, a gritty substance made of silicon crystals, could be used for preparing the surfaces of metal plates by scratching or roughening them. Together with fellow artists Michael Gallagher and Hubert Mesibov, he developed an innovative printmaking technique using carborundum mezzotint instead of etching tools to shape copper print plates.

His work became well-known during the 1940s and 50s. As well as portraits, his art depicted contemporary issues reflecting the social evolution of Black people during the first half of the 20th century. During World War II (1939-1945), he created a series of prints with a patriotic theme.

Dox died in 1965 in New Jersey at the age of 71.

MADAM CJ WALKER (SARAH BREEDLOVE)

Hair Care System

Sarah Breedlove was an entrepreneur who invented a hair care system.

Born in 1867 in Louisiana, US, she was orphaned at the age of seven and sent to live with her sister and brother-in-law. They moved to Mississippi in 1877, but she ran away at the age of 14 and went to Missouri, where her brothers had established themselves as barbers. She worked as a washerwoman and attended night school whenever she could.

During the 1890s, Sarah developed a scalp disorder that caused her to lose some of her hair. She began experimenting with home remedies and hair care treatments to try to help with her condition.

In 1905, she was hired as a sales agent by Annie Minerva Turnbo Malone (see contents page), a successful Black entrepreneur in hair care. Sarah moved to Colorado and later created her own specialised hair care products for Black people, called the 'Walker System'. Her husband, Charles J Walker, worked in advertising and helped to promote her hair care business, encouraging her to use the name Madam CJ Walker professionally.

She promoted her products by travelling around the country and giving lecture demonstrations on her formula for hair pomade, hair brushing, and the use of heated combs. In 1908, she established Madame CJ Walker Laboratories to manufacture beauty products and train sales beauticians. She was one of the first Black women to become a self-made millionaire and was known for her charitable work and educational efforts among Black people.

Madam CJ Walker died in 1919 in New York at the age of 51.

MOSES FLEETWOOD WALKER

Film Reel Loading and Changing (improvement)

Moses Fleetwood Walker was a professional baseball player and entrepreneur who developed improvements in film reel loading and changing.

Often known as Fleet, Moses was born in 1857 in Ohio, US. He joined Oberlin College in Ohio in 1878 and played on their baseball team. After a year, he left to play baseball for the University of Michigan, where he studied law.

He earned a living as a defensive catcher for various baseball teams, including the Toledo Blue Stockings in the Northwestern League, which moved from minor to major league level when they joined the American Association of Professional Baseball in 1884. Moses was the first Black man to play Major League Baseball.

He started inventing, and in 1891, he received a patent for an artillery shell that would explode once it had reached its target. In 1902, he and his brother began publishing *The Equator*, a Black-issues newspaper. In 1908, he published a book called *Our Home Colony: A Treatise on the Past, Present and Future of the Negro Race in America*.

Moses also successfully managed a hotel and an opera house theatre in Ohio, where he organised live entertainment and motion pictures or films, which was a new medium at the time. This led to his three improvements in film reel loading and changing, for which he received patents. His inventions helped to alert the screen projectionist when the film reel on one machine needed changing at the end of the reel, and a readily-loaded second machine could be started to avoid interrupting the film.

He died in 1924 in Ohio at the age of 67.

JAMES EDWARD MACEO WEST

Electret Microphone

Dr James Edward Maceo West is an acoustic engineer
who co-invented the electret microphone (which converts sound
into an electrical signal and is used in a wide range of electronic
products).

James was born in 1931 in Virginia, US. As a child, he became interested in finding out how things worked and enjoyed taking appliances apart to study them. He was fascinated by electricity and knew that he wanted to study science. He earned his bachelor's degree in physics at Temple University in Pennsylvania in 1957.

He began working at Bell Laboratories, a large research company that develops a wide range of new technologies. Together with fellow engineer Gerhard Sessler, he developed an inexpensive, highly sensitive and compact electret microphone in 1962, which relied on their invention of the electret transducer, a device that converts energy from one form to another. By 1968, their electret microphone was in mass production and used in telephones, tape recorders, hearing aids, camcorders, and baby monitors. Today the majority of contemporary microphones use their technology.

In 1997, he was appointed president-elect of the Acoustical Society of America and joined the National Academy of Engineering in 1998. He has worked with initiatives encouraging Black students and women to explore and pursue careers in science and technology. He later became a research professor in electrical and computer engineering at Johns Hopkins University in Maryland.

During his career, James received many awards and developed more than 200 patents. He has written a number of scientific papers and books and has received honorary doctorates from a number of universities.

CATHERINE (KATE) SPECK WICKS

Potato Crisps

Catherine Speck Wicks was a restaurant cook who invented potato crisps.

Catherine, who was known as Kate, was born in 1822. She was a cook at the Lake House Restaurant in New York at the time of her invention when she sliced up a sliver of potato that accidentally fell into a hot frying pan. Her brother, George 'Crum' Speck (1822-1914), tasted it, and his enthusiastic approval led the owner of the Lake House Restaurant to serve the crisps at the restaurant. They called it the 'Saratoga chip'.

George worked at the same restaurant as Kate, and is often credited as the inventor of the potato crisp instead. In the 1860s, he opened his own restaurant in New York, where he served a basket of potato crisps at every table. They were considered a delicacy, and his restaurant, called Crums, was very popular.

Unfortunately, neither Kate nor George thought to apply for a patent for the crisps. In the 1920s, a travelling salesman and entrepreneur named Herman Lay mass-produced the crisps, introducing them to communities all over the country, which was the beginnings of Lay's potato chips in the US today.

Kate died in 1924 in New York at the age of 102, and her obituary identifies her as the inventor of the famous Saratoga chips.

GRANVILLE TAILER WOODS

Multiplex or Inductor Telegraph

Granville Tailer Woods was an engineer who invented the multiplex or inductor telegraph, which sent messages between train stations and trains.

Born in 1856 in Ohio, US, Granville received little schooling and worked in a variety of jobs from a young age – as a machine operator, blacksmith, and fireman. He later studied engineering and electronics at night school and through private tutoring.

His most important invention was the multiplex or inductor telegraph in 1887, which allowed communications by voice over telegraph wires between train stations and moving trains. This helped to speed up important communications, preventing errors and accidents on railway tracks.

Granville defeated a lawsuit by famous inventor Thomas Edison, which challenged the patent for his invention. He later turned down Edison's offer to make him a partner in the Edison Electric Light Company, which created a range of electrical products. Thereafter, he became known as the 'Black Edison'. His patent was bought by another famous inventor, Alexander Graham Bell, and the payment allowed him to spend his time on research work.

Granville registered nearly 60 patents in his lifetime and founded his own company, the Woods Electric Company, to develop, manufacture, and sell electrical devices to help modernise railway services. His next most important invention was the power pick-up device in 1901, which formed the basis for the third rail used by electric-powered train systems today.

Many of his inventions were assigned to major manufacturers of electrical equipment and are part of much of today's daily life. If an inventor does not manufacture their invention, the patent can assigned or sold to be manufactured by someone else.

He died in 1910 in New York at the age of 53.

JANE COOKE WRIGHT

Chemotherapy and Cancer Treatment

Dr Jane Cooke Wright was an oncologist surgeon and pioneering researcher in chemotherapy and modern cancer treatment.

Jane was born in 1919 in New York, US. She came from a family of doctors and earned her medical degree in 1945 at the New York Medical College. In 1949, she joined her father at the Cancer Research Foundation in Harlem Hospital in New York, which he had established. Chemotherapy was still mainly experimental at the time, and she made numerous improvements to the treatment, including using nitrogen mustard agents to treat sarcoma, leukaemia, and lymphoma (types of cancer).

As an oncologist surgeon, Jane removed tumours (lumps of tissue in the body that may be cancerous) during surgery. She pioneered the use of patient tumour biopsies for drug testing against various tumours and developed a non-surgical procedure to deliver chemotherapy drugs to previously unreachable tumours in patients' kidneys and spleens. Her work revolutionised cancer research and how doctors treat cancer today.

In 1952, she was appointed director of the Cancer Research Foundation, and in 1955, she was named director of cancer chemotherapy research at the New York University Medical Centre. In 1964, she was the only Black person and the only woman among the founders of the American Society of Clinical Oncology. She held many other distinguished positions and received many awards in her lifetime.

Jane died in 2013 in New Jersey at the age of 93.

ARTHUR ZANG

Cardiopad

Arthur Zang invented the Cardiopad, a device that takes readings from patients' hearts and sends them to heart specialists for analysis and diagnosis.

Born in 1987 in Cameroon, he attended the Polytechnic School of Yaounde in Cameroon, where he studied computer engineering.

During his college education, Arthur was working at the local hospital when he discovered that there were only 30 cardiologists (heart specialists) in a country of more than 20 million people. This led to his invention of the Cardiopad, a touchscreen medical tablet that makes it possible for health workers to give heart examinations in rural areas that are far away from the cities in which cardiologists are normally based.

The Cardiopad transfers the results through mobile phone networks to cardiologists in less than 30 minutes, which saves time and allows for affordable treatment options. Cardiologists can examine the readings from wherever they are based and can send back digital reports of the patients' results. Any medical prescriptions needed are then sent to local clinics for the patients. The Cardiopad helps to save lives by connecting patients and cardiologists without the need to, and expense of, travel.

Arthur's invention was a personal venture. He had lost his uncle to cardiovascular disease, a heart condition, and grew up in a remote village where people could not easily receive healthcare. It was his continuous search for a solution that led him to develop the Cardiopad.

His invention was awarded the Africa Prize for Engineering Innovation by the UK's Royal Academy of Engineering in 2016.

About the Author

Joy James lives in London with her family. She works at a university and recently started writing non-fiction children's books to help educate and inform curious, young minds.

Acknowledgements

Thanks to Irine Parvin who was a joy to work with, for her lovely illustrations; Elise Abram who edited my manuscript, for her encouraging words and feedback; Daniella Blechner, Book Journey Mentor, for her help and advice throughout; and the rest of the team at Conscious Dreams Publishing.

Sources

1881 Institute, The. the1881institute.org.

Academic Dictionaries and Encyclopedias. enacademic.com.

Academic Kids Encyclopedia. academickids.com.

Academy of Robotics. academyofrobotics.co.uk.

Access Creative College. accesscreative.ac.uk.

African American Registry. aaregistry.org.

Alchetron. alchetron.com.

Alliance For AI. alliance4ai.org.

American Association of State Highway and Transportation Officials. transportation.org.

American Champions 365. americanchampions365.com.

American Chemical Society. acs.org.

American Institute of Chemical Engineers. aiche.org.

American Institute of Physics. aip.org.

American National Biography. anb.org.

American Society for Clinical Pathology. ascp.org.

Annie Malone Historical Society. anniemalonehistoricalsociety.org.

Antibiotic Research UK. antibioticresearch.org.uk.

Arizona State University. asu.edu.

Association of American Medical Colleges. aamc.org.

Association of Women Inventors & Entrepreneurs. inventingatoz.com.

Baltimore Museum of Art, The. artbma.org.

Bashen Corporation. bashencorp.com.

Beall, Miranda. *Valerie L Thomas Retires.* Volume 11, Number 3. National Aeronautics and Space Administration Space Science Data Coordinated Archive. nssdc.gsfc.nasa.gov. September 1995.

Binghamton University. Binghamton.edu.

Biography.com *Editors. Mark Dean (1957-).* Biography.com. biography.com. Updated 13 January 2021.

Birmingham Community Healthcare NHS Foundation Trust. bhamcommunity.nhs.uk.

Black America Web. blackamericaweb.com.

Black Doctor Org. blackdoctor.org.

Black Facts. blackfacts.com.

Black History Channel, The. theblackhistorychannel.com.

Black Inventor Online Museum, The. blackinventor.com.

Black Past. blackpast.org.

Black Then. blackthen.com.

BlackUSA. blackusa.com.

Board Game Geek. boardgamegeek.com.

Botswana Institute for Technology Research and Innovation. bitri.co.bw.

Brachman, *Steve. Dr Thomas Mensah: An innovator of fiber optics technologies.* IPWatchDog, ipwatchdog.com. February 2015.

Bridgeport Library History Center. bportlibrary.org.

Bridgewater State University. bridgew.edu.

British Broadcasting Corporation. *How to become a physicist: Mark Richards.* bbc.co.uk.

British Library, The. *Interview: Voices of Science: Mark Richards.* bl.uk.

Brooklyn Historic Railway Association. The. brooklynrail.net.

Brown University. brown.edu.

California State University, Stanislaus. csustan.edu.

Campbell House Museum. campbellhousemuseum.org.

Canadian Encyclopedia, The. thecanadianencyclopedia.ca.

Capitol Technology University. captechu.edu.

Caribbean Associations Group. cag-reading.org.uk.

Caribbean Elections. caribbeanelections.com.

Carillon Historical Park. daytonhistory.org.

Center for Applied Special Technology. cast.org.

Center of Science and Industry. cosi.org.

Chimtom, Ngala Killian. *Cameroonian inventor wins prize for handheld tablet bringing medicine to rural areas.* Cable Network News. edition.cnn.com. Updated 27 October 2017.

Clark Atlanta University. cau.edu.

Columbia University. columbia.edu.

Congressional Black Caucus Foundation. cbcfinc.org.

Consortium on the History of African Americans in the Medical Professions Resources. chaamp. virginia.edu.

Davis, Nicola. *Interview: Maggie Aderin-Pocock: how a space-obsessed schoolgirl battled the odds to become a top scientist.* The Guardian; The Observer. 21 September 2014.

DePauw University. depauw.edu.

Detroit Historical Society. detroithistorical.org.

Doughty, Melissa. *Let thy food be thy medicine.* Trinidad & Tobago Guardian. Guardian.co.tt. 24 September 2012.

Duke University Medical Center Archives. archives.mc.duke.edu.

Earl S Bell. earlsbell.com.

Ecofin Agency. agenceecofin.com.

Edison Electric Institute. eei.org.

Education Trust, The. edtrust.org.

Elayadathusseril, Gloria. *Isa and Amina Odidi are successful pharmaceutical entrepreneurs.* Canadian Immigrant Magazine. canadianimmigrant.ca. 29 May 2011.

Encyclopedia. encyclopedia.com.

Encyclopedia of Alabama. encyclopediaofalabama.org.

Encyclopedia Britannica. britannica.com.

Encyclopedia of Greater Philadelphia, The. philadelphiaencyclopedia.org.

Encyclopedia of World Biography. notablebiographies.com.

English Heritage. english-heritage.org.uk.

European Patent Office. epo.org.

Face2Face Africa. face2faceafrica.com.

Ferris State University. ferris.edu.

Florence Nightingale Museum London. florence-nightingale.co.uk.

Florida Agricultural and Mechanical University. famu.edu.

Forbes Woman Africa. *Thato Kgatlhanye, 23: CEO, Rethaka.* Forbes. forbesafrica.com. 1 February 2016.

Fort Wayne Museum of Art. fwmoa.org.

Foundation of Economic Education. fee.org.

Fourtane, Susan. *The Complete List of Black American Inventors, Scientists, and Engineers That Changed the World – Part Two.* Interesting Engineering. interestingengineering.com. 24 May 2018.

Franklin Institute, The. fi.edu.

Georgia Public Broadcasting. gpb.org.

Global African Diaspora Development Network. gaddn.org.

Goldsmiths, University of London. gold.ac.uk.

Gongali Model Co Ltd. gongalimodel.com.

Google Patents. patents.google.com.

Gotham Center for New York City History, The. gothamcenter.org.

Government Communication and Information System. gcis.gov.za.

Governors State University. govst.edu.

Gramma's Food. grammaeshop.com.

Harvard Radcliffe Institute. radcliffe.harvard.edu.

Henry Ford Museum of American Innovation. thehenryford.org.

Heriot-Watt University. hw.ac.uk.

History Channel. history.com.

HistoryMakers, *The. Interview: Jesse Russell, Sr.* thehistorymakers.org. 16 May 2012.

Howard University Libraries. howard.edu.

Hyde Collection. The. hydecollection.org.

Imperial College London. imperial.ac.uk.

Indiana Historical Society. indianahistory.org.

Indiana University Bloomington. Indiana.edu.

Infoplease. infoplease.com.

Institute of Electrical and Electronics Engineers. ieee.org.

Institute of Engineering and Technology, The. theiet.org.

Intellectual Property Owners Education Foundation. ipoef.org.

Intellipharmaceutics International Inc. intellipharmaceutics.com.

Interesting Engineering. interestingengineering.com.

IP Australia. ipaustralia.gov.au.

IP WatchDog. ipwatchdog.com.

Jackson Laboratory, The. jax.org.

James B Duke Memorial Library, Johnson C Smith University Library. library.jcsu.edu.

Jewell, Catherine. *Tanzanian entrepreneur develops innovative water filter*. WIPO Magazine. wipo.int. August 2015.

John Hopkins Whiting School of Engineering. engineering.jhu.edu.

Johnson Battery Technologies. johnsonbatterytech.com.

Johnson Collection, The. thejohnsoncollection.org.

Johnson Research and Development Co Inc. johnsonrd.com.

Justia Patents. patents.justia.com.

Kansas State University. k-state.edu.

Kansas State University College of Education. coe.k-state.edu.

Kreol International Magazine Editor. *Dolly Nicholas: Trinidad-born Chemist is Full of Ideas*. kreolmagazine.com. 12 October 2017.

Lemelson Center for the Study of Invention and Innovation. invention.si.edu.

Lemelson-Massachusetts Institute of Technology Program. *Joanna Hardin: CompUrest Keyboard Stand*. lemelson.mit.edu

Lewis Latimer House Museum. lewislatimerhouse.org.

Lewis Latimer Society and Museum. lewislatimersocietyandmuseum.org.

Liberty Science Center. lsc.org.

Library of Congress. loc.gov.

Lonnie Johnson. lonniejohnson.com.

McFadden, Christopher. Interesting Engineering. *The Complete List of Genius Black American Inventors, Scientists and Engineers – Part One*. Interesting Engineering. interestingengineering.com. 4 May 2018.

Mahoney, Eleanor. *Betty Wright Harris (1940-)*. BlackPast. blackpast.org. 27 January 2018.

Markovitz, Gayle. *The woman who created the technology behind internet calls explains what it takes to innovate*. World Economic Forum. weforum.org. 19 November 2020.

Mary Seacole Trust. maryseacoletrust.org.uk.

Minnesota Historical Society. mnhs.org.

Minor League Baseball. milb.com.

Minnesota Science and Technology Hall of Fame. msthalloffame.org.

Mississippi Encyclopedia Online. mississippiencyclopedia.org.

Museum of Food and Drink. mofad.org.

National Academies of Sciences; African American History Program. *James Edward West (1931-)*. cpnas.org.

National Academy of Engineering. nae.edu.

National Academy of Inventors. academyofinventors.org.

National Aeronautics and Space Administration. nasa.gov.

National Archives Foundation. archivesfoundation.org.

National Archives and Records Administration. archives.gov.

National Institute of Higher Education, Research, Science and Technology. *Dolly Nicholas*. icons. niherst.gov.tt.

National Institutes of Health. nih.gov.

National Inventors Hall of Fame. invent.org.

National Museum of African American History and Culture. nmaahc.si.edu.

National Park Service. nps.gov.

National Postal Museum. postalmuseum.si.edu,

National Science & Technology Medals Foundation. nationalmedals.org.

National Society of Black Physicists. nsbp.org.

National Women's History Museum. womenshistory.org.

Negro Leagues Baseball Museum. nlbm.com.

Nelson Mandela African Institution of Science and Technology, The. nm-aist.ac.tz.

New Jersey Chamber of Commerce. njchamber.com.

New Jersey Institute of Technology. njit.edu.

New York Medical College. nymc.edu.

New Zimbabwe News. *William Sachiti: Zimbabwean entrepreneur invents open-sourced technology to improve access to education in Africa*. newzimbabwe.com. 2 February 2020.

NCpedia. ncpedia.org.

Nubian Jak. nubianjak.org.

Nursing Theory. nursing-theory.org.

Oak Park River Forest Museum. oprfmuseum.org.

Ohio History Central. ohiohistorycentral.org.

Ohio State University Libraries, The. library.osu.edu.

Optical Society, The. *In Memoriam: Patricia Bath*, 1942-2019. osa.org. 30 May 2019.

Oregon State University. oregonstate.edu.

Patent and Trademark Resource Center Association. ptrca.org.

People Pill. peoplepill.com.

Philadelphia Museum of Art. philamuseum.org.

Philip Emeagwali. emeagwali.com.

Plastics Industry Association. plasticsindustry.org.

Public Broadcasting Service. pbs.org.

Reach Society. reachsociety.com.

ReadWorks. readworks.org.

Remember The 400 Foundation. rememberthe400.com.

Rhode Island College. ric.edu.

Royal Academy of Engineering, The. raeng.org.uk.

Royal College of Nursing, The. rcn.org.uk.

Royal Society, The. royalsociety.org.

Royal Society of Chemistry, The. rsc.org.

Rutgers University School of Arts and Sciences. sas.rutgers.edu.

San Diego Horticultural Society. sdhort.org.

Saratoga County Historical Society at Brookside Museum. brooksidemuseum.com.

School of the Art Institute of Chicago. saic.edu.

Science History Institute. sciencehistory.org.

Seattle Department of Transportation. seattle.gov/transportation.

Seeley G Mudd Library, Lawrence University. lawrence.edu/library.

Sephius 1. *African American Scientists and Inventors: Michael Croslin.* Daily Kos. dailykos.com. 4 April 2014.

Society for American Baseball Research. sabr.org.

Splash. *Bell, Earl S (Inventor, Architect, Entrepreneur and More).* Urban Areas. urbanareas.net. 2015.

State Historical Society of Missouri, The. shsmo.org.

Stratton House Inn. strattonhouse.com.

Strong National Museum of Play, The. museumofplay.org.

Sustainable Nanotechnology Organisation. susnano.org.

tEQuitable. tequitable.com.

ThoughtCo. thoughtco.com.

Traveling Black Inventions Museum, The. the blackinventionsmuseum.org.

Tuskegee University. tuskegee.edu.

UK Intellectual Property Office. gov.uk/government/organisations/intellectual-property-office.

US Army. army.mil.

US Department of Agriculture. usda.gov.

US Department of Education. ed.gov.

US Department of Energy. energy.gov.

US Department of Transportation. transportation.gov.

US Golf Association. usga.org.

US Patent and Trademark Office. uspto.gov.

University of California Los Angeles. ucla.edu.

University of California San Diego Library. library.ucsd.edu.

University of Central Florida. ucf.edu.

University of Edinburgh Alumni Services. *Geoff Palmer.* ed.ac.uk.

University of Energy and Natural Resources. uenr.edu.gh.

University of Georgia. uga.edu.

University of Glasgow. gla.ac.uk.

University of Houston. uh.edu.

University of Illinois at Urbana-Champaigne. illinois.edu.

University of Leicester. le.ac.uk.

University of Massachusetts Amherst. umass.edu.

University of Pennsylvania. upenn.edu.

University of South Florida. usf.edu.

University of Tennessee, Knoxville, The. utk.edu.

Virgin StartUp. *Reggae Reggae Sauce: From Notting Hill Carnival to Nationwide Supermarket Shelves*. virginstartup.org.

Walton Centre NHS Foundation Trust, The. thewaltoncentre.nhs.uk.

Washington State Commission on African American Affairs. caa.wa.gov.

Wharton School of the University of Pennsylvania, The. wharton.upenn.edu.

Williams, Scott. *Astronomers of the African Diaspora: George R Carruthers*. State University of New York at Buffalo. math.buffalo.edu.

Williams, Scott. *Astronomers of the African Diaspora: George R Carruthers*. State University of New York at Buffalo. math.buffalo.edu.

World Health Organisation. who.int.

World Intellectual Property Organisation. wipo.int.

Yarlagadda, Tara. *Jerry Lawson Forever Changed the Video Game Industry. How Stuff Works*. science.howstuffworks.com. 23 July 2020.

Your Dictionary. yourdictionary.com.

Zhana. *Black Success Stories; Chapter 3; Jak Dodd*. Zhana Books. 2006.

Conscious Dreams
P U B L I S H I N G

Be the author of your own destiny

www www.consciousdreamspublishing.com

✉ info@consciousdreamspublishing.com

Let's connect

CPSIA information can be obtained
at www.ICGtesting.com
Printed in the USA
LVHW071944270222
712157LV00005B/69

9 781913 674397